A GUIDE TO BECOMING A SCHOLARLY
PRACTITIONER IN STUDENT AFFAIRS

A GUIDE TO BECOMING A SCHOLARLY PRACTITIONER IN STUDENT AFFAIRS

Lisa J. Hatfield and Vicki L. Wise

Foreword by
Kevin Kruger

STERLING, VIRGINIA

Published by Stylus Publishing, LLC
22883 Quicksilver Drive
Sterling, Virginia 20166-2102

Library of Congress Cataloging-in-Publication Data
Hatfield, Lisa J.
  A guide to becoming a scholarly practitioner in student affairs /
Lisa J. Hatfield and Vicki L. Wise.
    pages cm
Includes bibliographical references and index.
ISBN 978-1-62036-151-1 (cloth : alk. paper)
ISBN 978-1-62036-152-8 (pbk. : alk. paper)
ISBN 978-1-62036-153-5 (library networkable e-edition)
ISBN 978-1-62036-154-2 (consumer e-edition)
1. Student affairs administrators. 2. Education--Research.
3. College students--Social conditions. I. Wise, Vicki L. II. Title.
LB2342.9.H38 2015
378.1'97--dc23
                                                            2014032808
13-digit ISBN: 978-1-62036-151-1 (cloth)
13-digit ISBN: 978-1-62036-152-8 (paperback)
13-digit ISBN: 978-1-62036-153-5 (library networkable e-edition)
13-digit ISBN: 978-1-62036-154-2 (consumer e-edition)

Cover designer: Laura Augustine

Printed in the United States of America

All first editions printed on acid-free paper
that meets the American National Standards Institute
Z39-48 Standard.

First Edition, 2015

10 9 8 7 6 5 4 3 2

To Yunji, may you remain as curious as you are today.
—LJH

To current and future student affairs scholar
practitioners, may you find your voice.
—VLW

CONTENTS

I vividly recall, in my first graduate classes in college student development in the late 1970s, the ongoing debate about the extent to which student affairs was considered a profession or simply a collection of roles and responsibilities that works with college students. The article "Student Personnel Work: A Profession Stillborn" (Penny, 1969) was often cited as representing the position that student affairs was not a profession.

> Student personnel workers, their philosophy, and their goals are not among the major influences today in colleges and universities. Analysis suggests . . . the conclusion that the occupation is not truly a profession and is not moving toward becoming one. Striking is the observation that there is a paucity of basic literature in the field. (p. 958)

Since that pessimistic assessment, there has developed a more widespread consensus that student affairs is a profession supported by a solid theoretical foundation and credible research. Seminal documents such as the 1987 "A Perspective on Student Affairs: A Statement Issued on the 50th Anniversary of the Student Personnel Point of View" called for student affairs professionals to develop "knowledge about human growth and development and how environments shape student behavior" (National Association of Student Personnel Administrators [NASPA], 1987, p. 11). The 1998 "Principles of Good Practice for Student Affairs" further expanded on this by stating that "knowledge of and ability to analyze research about students and their learning are critical components of good student affairs practice" (American College Personnel Association [ACPA] & NASPA, 1998, p. 4).

More recently the Task Force on the Future of Student Affairs reviewed a range of key documents and found five key themes common in student affairs work:

1. defining the nature of student affairs work;
2. developing and expanding theories and research to inform practice;
3. responding to, and increasing, the diversity of students;
4. demonstrating accountability for student learning and success; and
5. designing and ensuring professional development for effective student affairs practice. (ACPA & NASPA, 2010, p. 2)

These themes outline a framework from which to support research, assessment, and professional development in student affairs. In particular, the emergence of assessment as a key student affairs function has expanded research from being primarily a faculty-led initiative to being a critical component of most student affairs divisions. A national focus on the assessment of student learning and the growing demand for accountability by multiple stakeholders has resulted in a significant expansion of research and assessment in student affairs.

The last decade has also seen a significant increase in opportunities to publish within student affairs. Within the two primary student affairs associations, NASPA and ACPA, there are currently four refereed scholarly journals. NASPA publishes the *Journal of Student Affairs Research and Practice* (*JSARP*), the *Journal of College and Character* (*JCC*), and the *NASPA Journal about Women in Higher Education* (*NJAWE*), and ACPA publishes the *Journal of College Student Development*. Other student affairs associations such as Association of College Unions International (ACUI), Association of College and University Housing Officers-International (ACUHO-I), and the Association for Student Conduct Administration (ASCA) have also developed new journals and publications that provide writing opportunities.

It is worth noting that within the last 10 years new writing and publication venues have emerged in the form of online blogs and newsletters. There is a growing list of student affairs blogs that are more applied and opinion-editorial in nature, rather than research and theoretical in substance. However, these blogs allow for dialogue and commentary on contemporary issues that do contribute to the literature of the student affairs profession. In the same way blogs and online resources have transformed the news and media business, it is likely that these same tools will continue to advance and inform student affairs practice.

This book provides a valuable foundation and exploration of the research, publication, and presentation opportunities that have been identified as so important to the student affairs profession. These activities contribute to our overall knowledge about student learning and our understanding of the factors that contribute to student success, degree progress, and persistence. In addition, assessment, evaluation, and research have been identified as core competencies for all student affairs professionals (ACPA & NASPA, 2010). The practical guidance contained in this book will be useful for professionals at all levels of their professional development.

Kevin Kruger
President
NASPA - Student Affairs Administrators in Higher Education

References

ACPA & NASPA. (1998). *Principles of good practice for student affairs*. Washington, DC: Author.

ACPA & NASPA, Task Force on the Future of Student Affairs. (2010). *Envisioning the future of student affairs*. Washington, DC: Author.

ACPA & NASPA. *Professional competency areas for student affairs practitioners*. Washington, DC: Author.

NASPA. (1990). *Standards of professional practice*. Retrieved from NASPA website: https://www.naspa.org/about/student-affairs

NASPA. (1987). *A perspective on student affairs: A statement issued on the 50th anniversary of the student personnel point of view*. Washington, DC: Author.

Penny, J. F. (1969). Student personnel work: A profession stillborn. *Personnel and Guidance Journal, 47*(10), 958–962. doi: 10.1002/j.2164-4918.1969.tb02879.x

INTRODUCTION

We wrote this book because we believe that student affairs professionals have valuable things to say. Many student affairs professionals, however, do not know how to go about getting their voices heard. As a result, we want to demystify the presentation and publication process so that these individuals will feel confident in doing both, thus contributing to their agency and professional growth. We also hope this book will contribute positively to student experiences as student affairs professionals share more of their successful practices and research.

This book is intended for all levels of professionals in student affairs. We hope that it plants the seed of scholarship in new professionals as they learn to navigate their roles and institutions, that it inspires midlevel professionals to present or write about the myriad of experiences they have had, and that it prompts senior administrators to pursue their own scholarship as well as create a supportive environment for their staff to do so.

We wanted to create a practical guide for those desiring to present or publish. We also thought it necessary to give some background on what we see as a lack of scholarship production and to provide the impetus for a movement to not only collaborate with our colleagues in academic affairs but also produce our own research and scholarly work. Because of the applicable nature of this book, we give lots of advice about writing, speaking, and how to stay on task. We know that there are numerous books and online resources that can help you with all of these areas, so we chose not to repeat much of what can easily be found elsewhere. We do suggest several of these resources in the context of this book and encourage you to use them.

This book would not have been possible without the immense time and positive energy given us from the following people: Dan Fortmiller, Jackie Balzer, Karen Haley, and J. R. Tarrabochia. A special thank-you goes to Dannelle Stevens for making this book possible as well as John von Knorring at Stylus Publishing for his support and feedback. We would also like to thank our family and friends near and far for putting up with us throughout this process, especially John Hatfield, Yunji Hatfield, and Linda Leland.

Finally, we wish to acknowledge and thank the people we interviewed for this book—we learned a great deal from their collective wisdom: Laura Bayless, assistant vice chancellor for Student Affairs, University of

Wisconsin–Platteville; Doris Ching, emeritus vice president of Student Affairs, University of Hawai'i System; Michael Christakis, associate vice president for Student Success and public service professor, University at Albany, State University of New York; Zebulun Davenport, vice chancellor for Student Affairs, Indiana University–Purdue University Indianapolis; Kathleen Kerr, executive director of Residence Life & Housing, University of Delaware; Jennifer Massey, assistant dean for Student Learning & Engagement, Baylor University; Michael Segawa, vice president for Student Affairs and dean of students, University of Puget Sound; and Frank Shushok Jr., senior associate vice president for Student Affairs and associate professor of higher education, Virginia Tech.

I

WHY STUDENT AFFAIRS PROFESSIONALS SHOULD PURSUE SCHOLARSHIP (AND WHY WE DON'T)

During your first appointment of the day, an international student weeps in your office because this system called U.S. higher education is so strange to her. You hand her a tissue before you can even savor the first sip of your morning coffee. At the same time, your colleague across campus is trying to figure out how to create a field for preferred names in the student information system because transgender students have requested this. And as the clock barely reaches 9 a.m., the veterans services director has been on hold for the past 30 minutes with the federal government. When, during this or any similar morning, does a student affairs professional have time to even think about putting together a conference presentation or writing a paper for publication?

For many reasons, including the examples just given of the "tyranny of the urgent" (Sriram, 2011, p. 1), student affairs professionals don't pursue scholarship created through presenting and publishing. Saunders, Register, Cooper, Bates, and Daddona (2000) concluded that the profession of student affairs has seen a decrease in scholarship by administrators. This book, we hope, will help those very people who should be sharing their experiences to further the knowledge and practices that will ultimately help students. We are writing this book because we believe in the value of student affairs professionals viewing themselves as scholar practitioners.

What is a *scholar practitioner*? Kidder (2010) defines such a person as one who "engages in research and scholarly endeavors while continuing in the role of an administrator" (p. 1). To become a scholar practitioner, Schroeder and Pike (2001) insist that the fundamental question to ask is this: What should an individual know and be able to do with this knowledge in order to be effective? In other words, how can scholarship be applied to the practicalities of student experiences?

This book is intended for beginning professionals, those in their mid-careers, and even senior student affairs administrators who have had many years to reflect on the profession itself and their personal journeys through it. We use the words *professionals* and *practitioners* interchangeably, and we also refer to *administrators* knowing that not all those in student affairs view themselves as such. However, most of what is offered in this book can be applied to all student affairs professionals regardless of their title or years in the profession.

The Push for Scholarship

It isn't enough to say we want a professional to become a scholar practitioner. We need to share why it's important to identify as one. Scholarship is leadership and takes us from practice to influencing the field of student affairs. Allen (2002) posits,

> Leadership involves fulfilling seven different roles that help practitioners make meaning of their work, increase their understanding of the whole system, identify key relationships within our practice, connect the past with the present and the future, identify what is missing in the present and articulate alternate visions of our future, identify emergent practices and theories, and create connective wisdom for the field. (pp. 149–150)

෨෬

Scholarship is leadership and takes us from practice to influencing the field of student affairs.

෨෬

In *Scholarship Reconsidered*, Boyer (1990) calls for us to expand our understanding of what constitutes scholarship: "The work of the scholar means stepping back from one's investigation, looking for connections, building bridges between theory and practice, and communicating one's knowledge effectively to students" (p. 16). Moreover, Boyer offers a view of scholarship that calls for us to think of research beyond creation or discovery, and that is research of integration, application, and teaching.

Since 2001, the national student affairs organizations American College Personnel Association (ACPA) and NASPA, Student Affairs Administrators in Higher Education as well as their respective journals have explored topics on scholarship in student affairs. There has been a call for more scholarship and the expansion of our view of scholarship. And in 2006, NASPA held a summit on scholarship (Jablonski, Mena, Manning, Carpenter, & Siko, 2006) that has served as a catalyst for reframing scholarship in student affairs. Carpenter (2001) extended Boyer's work to student affairs and included the "scholarship of practice" (p. 183), calling on student affairs practitioners to use theory and scholarship in their daily interactions. In addition, both NASPA and ACPA jointly published *Professional Competency Areas for Student Affairs Practitioners* (ACPA & NASPA, 2010), which advocates using theories to inform our practice and contributing to the field through our reflections.

Student affairs scholar practitioners must hold fast to the idea of their own continual learning, which, in turn, further benefits students. This learning cannot occur without reflecting on one's own practice, attitudes, and mindset. According to Dewey (1910), "Active, persistent, and careful consideration of any belief or supposed form of knowledge in the light of the grounds that support it, and the further conclusions to which it tends, constitutes reflective thought" (p. 2). When we engage in reflection, we allow ourselves to question what happened in a given situation and to view the event from a contextual distance to determine whether we have experienced any growth. We must reflect critically, see ourselves as both teachers and learners, and come to know ourselves within the processes of research itself.

ℰℛ

We must reflect critically, see ourselves as both teachers and learners, and come to know ourselves within the processes of research itself.

ℰℛ

Yes, our voices are important, but we must be able to articulate *why* our voices are important for the profession to develop. How can we relate what happened to us and what we learned from it so our peers can benefit? In this sense, as student affairs professionals we must see ourselves as educators and teachers not only to the students we serve but also to our colleagues.

Dewey (1910) goes on to say that educators need to "cultivate deep-seated and effective habits of discriminating tested beliefs from mere assertions, guesses, and opinions" and to "develop a lively, sincere, and open-minded preference for conclusions that are properly grounded" (pp. 27–28). Student affairs professionals are in the best position to test the myths about what really works for students to have access to, persist in, and graduate from college. We experience daily how some policies, though well intended, don't always translate well to students. As "street-level bureaucrats" (Marshall & Gerstl-Pepin, 2005), we have developed, through our daily interactions with students, the grounding for the conclusions we draw of what works. In other words, we have much to share and offer in how we can improve this thing called college. Without scholarship, without presenting and writing, these stories and voices will be lost.

ℰℭ

Student affairs professionals are in the best position to test the myths about what really works for students to have access to, persist in, and graduate from college.

ℰℭ

Why We Don't Write

What keeps us from writing when we know how important it is for our own growth and for the health of the field? Student affairs professionals can blame the immediacy of our daily work for not identifying as scholar practitioners. But this may be too easy of a scapegoat. In this section we suggest several other reasons why we don't pursue scholarship. If we understand the causes, then we can strategize and do something about them.

Not Enough Reading

If we are not reading research, we are probably not contributing to it. Carpenter (2001) states, "Any student affairs professional not reading the literature, not becoming knowledgeable of research and theory, is not acting ethically. Students have a right to expect that student affairs professionals are knowledgeable of appropriate theories, current research, and proven best practices" (p. 311). More important, our practice must be guided by theory and research. Reading research provides practitioners with a solid foundation for developing and improving programs and services. It takes us beyond anecdotal knowing to knowing that has been examined, and it adds legitimacy and intention to our work.

ℰℭ

Reading research provides practitioners with a solid foundation for developing and improving programs and services.

ℰℭ

Not Expected of Positions and Not Valued

Unlike tenure-track faculty, student affairs practitioners do not have the same pressure to publish results of their impact on student learning and development. Studies show that supervisors give little incentive to student affairs practitioners to pursue scholarship (Fey & Carpenter, 1996; Saunders & Cooper, 1999); the reason for this may be that many midlevel managers in student affairs underutilize and undervalue assessment and research skills (Fey & Carpenter, 1996; Saunders & Cooper, 1999; Sermershein & Keim, 2005).

Second-Class Citizen Syndrome

Kimbrough (2007) suggests one reason that 85% of chief student affairs officers and nearly 48% of deans of students have terminal degrees may be that there is a "climate in higher education that has discounted the importance of student affairs work" (p. 278). Earning an advanced degree connotes, in part, a metaphorical membership in the academic community. Kuh and Banta (2000) noted cultural-historical barriers to a perceived lack of respect for student affairs professionals that grew partially from faculty historically being given tasks that they did not want to do, many of which were noncurricular. This resulted in faculty spending more time on research and scholarship and less time on what is now considered the realm of student affairs. Student affairs professionals may feel inferior to their colleagues in academic departments not only in degree obtainment but also in their research skills, and thus less likely to publicly share research through presentations or publications.

Inadequate Academic Preparation

Professional skills in reading and doing research are necessary for scholarly writing. Unfortunately, some graduate student affairs programs may not adequately prepare practitioners to write and publish. According to Jablonski et al. (2006), "Even students from some of our best programs are inadequately trained in research, evaluation, and assessment. Even when they are rudimentarily trained, they frequently lack a conception of the values of scholarship and their obligation to consume and contribute to research in the field" (p. 187). Furthermore, student affairs professionals who have been out of their graduate programs for a while may feel too distant to the research skills and thus less competent in their ability to do research and publish (Saunders et al., 2000; Schroeder & Pike, 2001).

Silos on Campus

When was the last time you ventured more than a few buildings away from your office? How about even down the hall? The university has become more fragmented (Boyer, 1990), which can lead to a lack of coherence in students' educational experiences. To foster a holistic student journey, rather than a "miscellaneous heap of separate bits of experience" (Dewey, 1902, p. 5), educators across the university need to be intentional in student learning. College, therefore, can be more of an accumulation of inextricably linked experiences and not separate, discrete entities. This intentionality can occur only when educators actually *talk* with each other. Building community often is a precursor to scholarship.

Lack of Motivation

The job descriptions of student affairs professionals typically don't include scholarship, unlike those of their peers in academic departments. If research and scholarship are not valued by supervisors (Fey & Carpenter, 1996; Saunders & Cooper, 1999) and staff are not expected to participate in such, it would not be surprising that there would be little motivation or incentive to engage (Schroeder & Pike, 2001).

Our Challenge to Student Affairs Professionals

You now know the importance of being a scholar practitioner, and you now understand better the reasons student affairs professionals might not engage in research and scholarship. Here is our question to you: If you could give voice to those who were marginalized, if you could change the field of student affairs through your voice, if you could create better collaborations across campus with our academic colleagues, and if you could share your insights with parents, students, and other invested stakeholders so that they will know what we contribute to student learning and development, why wouldn't you? Unless student affairs practitioners, those who work most closely with students, take the time to present or publish, changes to the field will not be informed by those most knowledgeable to improve practices, programs, and services. It is our hope that this book will provide the vehicle for you to engage in scholarship.

Structure of the Book: Much to Write About

We have organized this book with great intentionality. As you have read, we firmly believe that student affairs professionals need to identify as scholar practitioners to further the daily good work they are doing with students. For this reason, we spent the majority of this chapter sharing our thoughts about why presenting and publishing need to be priorities for all student affairs professionals regardless of title or years of experience.

In the chapters that follow, we provide helpful information about presenting and then move on to the world of publishing, including writing strategies to keep you going. We end with conversations with senior student affairs officers about scholarship in the profession.

Presenting at a conference may seem less daunting than submitting writing for publication, and, thus, we focus on this first. There are a variety of conferences—local, regional, national, and international—and those new to presenting may want to ease into it by submitting a proposal for a local or regional conference. Those more seasoned may desire to challenge themselves and pursue acceptance at national or international conferences. If you have the research bug (and research doesn't have to be in a lab or statistically overwhelming), you may just want to write that paper or book. Certainly, presenting and publishing are not mutually exclusive. Technology has afforded other modes of publishing, which we also discuss. The latter part of the book provides strategies to facilitate the presenting and publishing processes and offers stylistic writing guidelines. We are well aware that you may have a few of these texts on your shelf (or on your Kindle or bookmarked on your desktop). However, we offer these in one place for ease of use. We hope that new professionals through chief student affairs officers will use this book as a guide for their scholar practitioner selves throughout their careers.

But first, we'd like to talk about feedback. Why do we dedicate an entire chapter to feedback and why so early in the book? Well, do you like to be told how you can improve what you're doing? What are your recollections of getting a graded paper back in school or that annual evaluation at work? We hope that you have positive, happy thoughts associated with feedback, but we surmise that you, like most human beings, probably don't. As scholar practitioners, however, collegial feedback is a must. We invite you to read on.

2

WE LOVE FEEDBACK

Fear Feedback No More!

"A word of caution before you open the attachment—the article is heavily edited, but do not be discouraged by that," wrote the kindhearted reviewer who apparently had taken the first look at a paper one of us had submitted for publication. The reviewer continued, "I hope what I have already done for you in terms of editing will significantly cut down on the amount of time you would need to dedicate." Great. Not only was the paper *that* bad, but now I also had guilt on my conscience because this person had spent so much time making up for my errant ways. I quickly opened the document, scanned through it, noted the line-by-line comments, and closed it as fast as I could. The last thing I felt at that moment was openness to the glorious wonders of feedback.

A few days later, early in the morning when my brain is the most clear, I clicked on the document again. This time, I took a deep breath and started reading. Just as I had suspected, the comments were mostly correct. With my cup of coffee in hand, I began to tackle what I really knew all along wasn't my best work.

We have all experienced feedback in some form from key people in our lives, such as teachers, faculty, parents, family, and peers. And as we know, not all feedback occurs in the same way, depending on the intended response. Moreover, not all feedback is perceived as useful. So, what is useful feedback? Best practice in education dictates that students receive feedback about their performance on tasks if they are to improve both their performance and their understanding of the material (Bruning, Schraw, & Ronning, 1995; Upcraft & Schuh, 1996; Wiggins, 1998). Feedback "is an essential part of any completed learning" (Wiggins, 1998, p. 43).

&)C&

*Learning how to give and receive feedback is an
essential skill for effective communication.*

&)C&

Feedback can be as simple as a "correct" or an "incorrect" response, or, as in scholarly writing reviews, be detailed and constructive. What is common across those who give feedback is the intention of improving performance. Krathwohl (2009) likens ideas in scholarship to concentric circles that radiate out when an object is dropped in water. As the waves (ideas) move out, they touch other scholars, who give feedback, which strengthens the original work. "Both positive and negative reactions are welcome," states Krathwohl (2009, p. 38), because they help researchers think about what they have done, how they are thinking about it, and how to communicate their findings.

Feedback can be difficult because it contradicts the "cultural tradition that privileges the individual agent" and, in writing, the notion of the solitary author (Moore Howard, 2001, p. 55). It is a very Western belief that the individual needs to do all the work and receive all the glory. However, in writing there is the notion of collaborative pedagogy, which has roots in social constructivism, in which beliefs are socially justified and constructed in the community (Moore Howard, 2001). Collaborative learning builds on people's tendency to learn from each other when they wish to overcome common obstacles or grasp difficult concepts (Hobson, 2001). We need to become more comfortable with this idea of working with others whether in writing groups or in simply asking for feedback. This makes our writing vulnerable, but it's a lot easier to take feedback from a colleague than it is having a paper or conference proposal rejected. Not only is the end product most likely going to be better, but professional community is created in the process as well.

The Purpose of Feedback: How It Can Change Us as Writers

Learning how to give and receive feedback is an essential skill for effective communication because "writing should almost always be a communication between writer and reader, and therefore feedback is the best way to sample how that communication is developing" (The Royal Literary Fund, n.d.).

&)C&

*Feedback "is an essential part of any completed learning"
(Wiggins, 1998, p. 43).*

&)C&

ഇറര

*"Writing should almost always be a communication
between writer and reader, and therefore feedback is the
best way to sample how that communication is developing"
(The Royal Literary Fund, n.d.).*

ഇറര

We know that feedback is critical to improving the performance of writing, but it can be challenging to seek. Determining from whom and at what point to seek feedback is a great place to start. Seek feedback from colleagues while your writing is in draft form, but make sure to set some parameters around that feedback. Feedback needs to inform your practice, solicit feedback that will help you grow. For example, you might seek feedback from a colleague who shares expertise on your topic or a colleague who has great editing skills and can review your work for grammar and style. Ideally, feedback needs to remain positive, not artificial, and provide insights on the strength of your work as well as the areas for needed improvement. Wolcott (2001) states that we must "choose early reviewers with care and instruct them carefully as to the kind (and extent) of criticism you feel will be most helpful at each stage of your writing" (p. 62). Caffarella and Barnett (2000) found that doctoral students trained in receiving and giving critiques reported improved scholarly writing and improved confidence as academic writers. The students attributed personalized face-to-face feedback that is iterative and ongoing as key to these improvements.

ഇറര

*Feedback needs to inform your practice, solicit feedback that
will help you grow.*

ഇറര

Writing can be an emotional exercise; we invest much of ourselves in the process, and the processes of giving and receiving feedback can be stressful. By choosing colleagues for initial reviews, we have the opportunity to receive feedback that feels supportive. That said, there are times when even the closest of colleagues will provide feedback that stings. In the Caffarella and Barnett (2000) study, doctoral students reported that while the critiquing process was useful, it was also "highly emotional and at times frustrating" (p. 39).

How does one deal with the emotional aspects of giving and receiving feedback? We're reminded of Dweck's (2006) work with mindsets. According to Dweck (2006), human qualities such as intellectual skills can be cultivated through effort. For example, in her study, children were asked to put together a complicated puzzle. Those who felt this challenge as a positive experience weren't thinking they were failing; rather, they viewed this exercise as learning. They had a growth mindset, not a fixed one. Research has shown that people define *ability* in two diverse ways: (a) a fixed ability that needs to be proven and (b) a changeable ability that can be developed through learning (Dweck, 2006). Student affairs scholar practitioners need to have this latter mindset of ability as well. We must adhere to a growth mindset, one that can be molded through opportunities such as giving and receiving feedback on our work, including our writings.

What Type of Feedback Is Most Useful to the Writer?

One of us (Lisa) is a former high school language arts and journalism teacher and, during those years, learned of the Oregon writing standards used for what was then the state's Certificate of Initial Mastery program. We won't go into detail about the program here, but what is important was how it changed giving feedback for many teachers. Rather than marginalia (Did students really ever read these comments?), much feedback was given by rubrics in the following areas: content, organization, voice, sentence fluency, and conventions. Although these categories changed a bit over the years, they provided conversation points for the student writers' focused revisions and other future writings. Under each of the broad categories were details about what a proficient score means in organization or what a developing voice looks like. Variations of the rubrics are still in use today and can be found both in K–12 and in higher education.

   Using these rubrics created a common language for what was expected in the classroom. Students began to use this language when peer reviewing papers. And teachers didn't have to spend endless amounts of time writing comments on everything bad (and good, we hope) and noting every comma error. We could evaluate a paper in its entirety, or we could focus on content and organization first. Such language helped students see that revising a paper was more than "fixing" grammatical errors. More experienced writers tend to make content and organization changes, but graduate students, much like students in K–12, minimally use revision to change or improve ideas in their text (Torrance, Thomas, & Robinson, 1992). Once we had a solid working draft, with content and organizational revisions, we could then focus more on the editing.

   If you want quick feedback from a colleague without creating a rubric, here are some feedback request openers that have helped us as writers and readers:

- As a reader: "I especially liked . . ."; "I wanted to learn more about . . ."
- As a writer: "I would like feedback specifically about . . ."

It's important to note that you're not asking, "Is this a good paper?" What specifically does "good" mean? If you don't know, we suggest reviewing the language of various writing rubrics. Oregon's Department of Education uses a six-point writing rubric that scores ideas and content, organization, voice, word choice, sentence fluency, conventions, and citing sources. A rating of four for each trait generally has been determined as passing. (For Oregon's Department of Education rubric and its detailed language characterizing each level of the traits, see www.ode.state.or.us/wma/teachlearn/testing/scoring/guides/2011-12/wriscorguide_eng_no-dates.pdf.) Portland State University offers a holistic rubric through its general education program that also uses a six-point scale. (Portland State University's rubric can be found at www.pdx.edu/sites/www.pdx.edu.unst/files/unst_rubric_writing.pdf.)

ℰℛ

Criticism is always a bit painful to the ego, but when you receive it with the right mindset, your writing is sure to improve.

ℰℛ

If you still fear feedback, you're not alone. The key is not to be afraid of it but to embrace it head-on with a clear and open mind. Criticism is always a bit painful to the ego, but when you receive it with the right mindset, your writing is sure to improve.

3

THE PRESENTATION

Four of the five people who attended the first conference presentation one of us gave rated it pretty good. The overheads (yes, overheads) were graphically appropriate, the speaking voice was clear enough, and the organization was decently effective. The fifth attendee thought it was just okay. "How could we do anything with the data if we only studied three people?" he asked. Good question. He added that not enough information was shared about the participants, that the large room made the speaker's voice echo, and so on. The merits of quantitative and qualitative research aside, that lone dissenter was probably right. The presentation really didn't feel that great. In hindsight, it was a good thing that one participant was honest. How do you ensure that your next presentation is better than this one? Read on.

Presentations are a great way to get started on your way to becoming a scholar practitioner, and they're also important to those who have published a great deal. If you're thinking of sharing the good work you and your colleagues are doing at your institution or want to get the word out about your publication, go online to search for organizations that would benefit from learning about what you have to say. Where do you begin? All these conferences sound exciting, but your director can send you to only one. Where do you begin this presentation process? This chapter seeks to take you through the steps of finding the right conference and giving your best presentation. But first, we start, well, at the beginning: What is a presentation anyway?

❧❦

Presentations are a great way to get started on your way to becoming a scholar practitioner, and they're also important to those who have published a great deal.

❧❦

Hoff (1988) defines a *presentation* as a "commitment by the presenter to help the audience do something—and a constant, simultaneous evaluation of that commitment by the audience" (p. 7). A presentation is a live interchange between people. The audience desires to learn more about something, and the presenter ostensibly has what the audience hopes will meet their needs. "If truth be told," Hoff says, "the audience arrives on the scene with the ardent hope that the presenter knows something that it does not" (p. 9). In other words, it's not just you getting up at the front of the room and talking; it is, instead, a great deal of responsibility that the presenter must take seriously. We're not saying you can't have fun with your presentation (you can and should); rather, that fun needs to be part of the very serious work that goes into your preparation.

We explore first in this chapter what goes through the minds of many professionals who desire to add presentations to their professional repertoire: the dreaded fear of public speaking. We then speak to how to choose a conference. We spend the majority of this chapter sharing how the proposal process works and giving suggestions for good presentations.

What Are You Truly Afraid Of?

> According to most studies, people's number one fear is public speaking. Number two is death. Death is number two. Does that sound right? This means to the average person, if you go to a funeral, you're better off in the casket than doing the eulogy. (Seinfeld, 1998)

Although these are the words of a comedian, there is some truth that people fear public speaking. If you ever had to give a presentation and experienced dry mouth, heart palpitations, and upset stomach, you may be able to relate to this quote.

What are you truly afraid of? Is it rejection? Or perhaps failure? Is it that you'll trip over a cable or that your zipper will be down? If you pinpoint where your fear lies, you can choose to *do* something about that very specific fear. Besides, there might be value in that fear. Gregory (1999) cites speech teacher Elayne Snyder, who uses the term *positive nervousness* for that fear-driven adrenaline rush. This is the "zesty, enthusiastic, lively feeling with a slight edge to it. Positive nervousness is the state you'll achieve by converting your anxiety into constructive energy. . . . It's still nervousness but you're no longer victimized by it; instead you're vitalized by it" (p. 27). Other research shows that some anxiety can actually help improve your performance. Researchers have distinguished between facilitating and debilitating anxiety (Deci & Ryan, 1992). Facilitating anxiety occurs when we face a challenge in which we know we can succeed with some effort, and debilitating anxiety occurs when we believe we cannot succeed even with effort. You may want to recall Dweck's (2006) thoughts on mindset (also chapter 2 of this book) if the idea of presenting makes you anxious.

The keys to using anxiety to your best advantage are to have confidence that your work has value and to be prepared. Pick a topic to present for which you have a good understanding. What questions did you have about this topic that you were able to address and feel would be useful to others to know? What theoretical frameworks support your topic? Once you determine your topic, think about your audience and what they need to know. Remember, you have expertise they may not, so you want to treat your presentation as a teaching opportunity. If you feel uncertain venturing out on your own for the first time, consider copresenting as an option. In chapter 7, we provide some guidelines for presenting as a group. The next step is to prepare and then prepare some more. Create your presentation and then share it with trusted colleagues, and make sure to solicit honest feedback about ways you can improve your presentation (see chapter 2). It is always a good idea to time yourself to make sure you can present in the allotted time. By practicing, you will become very comfortable with your material and your confidence will increase. We talk more specifically about these areas later in this chapter.

How to Choose a Conference

Working in student affairs, we have so many conferences to choose from to share our work. If you have ever reviewed the Council for the Advancement of Standards in Higher Education (CAS) (2012), you know that there are 40 CAS member organizations represented in these standards and that many of these organizations have regional and national conferences. A complete list is located on the CAS website (www.cas.edu/index.php/about/members). Here is just a sampling of organizations that hold conferences in student affairs:

- NASPA (Student Affairs Administrators in Higher Education): aids in the advancement, health, and sustainability of the student affairs profession
- ACPA (American College Personnel Association): advances student affairs and engages students for a lifetime of learning and discovery
- NACADA (National Academic Advising Association): promotes the theory, delivery, application, and advancement of academic advising to enhance student learning and development
- NACA (National Association for Campus Activities): provides innovative practices and access to programs that support campus engagement

- ACUHO-I (Association of College and University Housing Officers–International): develops exceptional residential experiences at colleges, universities, and other postsecondary institutions around the world
- NODA (National Orientation Directors Association): provides education, leadership, and professional development in the fields of college student orientation, transition, and retention
- NIRSA (National Intramural-Recreational Sports Association): supports leaders in collegiate recreation

Select a conference that will allow you to feel most comfortable in presenting, especially if this is your first presentation. Regional conferences tend to be smaller, so that may be a great place to start. Another strategy for selecting a conference is to look online at the prior year's conference schedule. Are the topics presented interesting to you and do they inform your work? Also, if there are professional Listservs and/or social media sites you follow perhaps you can solicit feedback on conferences these professionals attend.

Types of Proposals

Now that you have selected your conference, how do you create your proposal? Almost all conferences have the same types of possibilities for presenting, including poster sessions, roundtables, panels, presentations (individual and group), and workshops. As you consider which type of proposal may be best, keep in mind what you want to do with your topic presentation. Ask yourself the following: Do you think you may want to publish an article about it? How would this type of presentation serve as a stepping-stone in that direction? We provide a brief description of each of these types of proposals, but it is best to go to the conference website to learn more about the requirements for submitting a proposal in each of these categories.

- *Poster Sessions.* These are a great opportunity to share your work with the entire conference audience and are designed to showcase interesting new approaches and practices that do not yet have the maturity of programs presented in concurrent sessions. In these sessions you can display visual charts, diagrams, pictures, and graphs that demonstrate key findings.
- *Roundtables.* These are facilitated discussions among colleagues whose papers share a common theme or offer participants an opportunity to share their comments about one paper per table. For the former, once they accept submissions for roundtables, the conference's program chairs cluster papers of similar topics at one table so that presenters

can get feedback from colleagues with like interests. Facilitators, who can be the paper's author if theirs is the only paper at a table, lead discussions on current topics, issues, and strategies.

- *Panels.* Panel presentations are similar to roundtables. Participants present short papers in an informal session. Typically a moderator or chair directs the session, ensuring that the presentations are focused and on track, and is responsible for promoting discussion with and soliciting feedback from the audience.
- *Presentations.* There are various forms of presentations. In some, each presentation is limited to the speaker's topic (and may involve the speaker's colleagues or collaborators presenting collectively as a group). In others, the session may involve the consecutive delivery of multiple papers, with a discussant concluding with scholarly feedback on all of them. Whether you present individually or in a group, presentations are an opportunity to provide research findings or overview of a model or program.
- *Workshops.* These provide participants an opportunity to engage the facilitator and each other in an extended learning session about a particular topic and apply it to their individual situations. Workshops typically occur at the beginning and/or end of conferences. In many conferences, attendees pay extra to participate in workshops, and workshops are seen as professional development, led by an expert on the topic. Workshops may run from half to a full day and typically include a mix of presenting with audience participation.
- *Out-of-box.* A promising new style of presenting called PechaKucha allows participants to showcase their work by presenting 20 slides for 20 seconds each (6 minutes and 40 seconds) and contains little text but high use of visuals. This format was used at the ACPA 2014 annual conference, and we expect to see more of it in the future.

What Makes a Good Presentation Topic?

Deciding on a presentation topic may be easier than you think. Examine what you do in your programs and services. What are you doing that others may benefit from knowing about? What are your program goals and outcomes, and how does what you have learned from your assessment of these contribute to your field? You should also think about the theories that undergird your practice and which ones you want to share. The lack of theoretical underpinnings is a concern for many scholar practitioners when it comes to conference presentations (we talk more about this in chapter 8). You will need to look at the theme of the conference to which you plan to submit your proposal and determine how your work fits into that theme.

There are many untapped and underrepresented areas of student affairs that are ripe for conference presentations. For example, at our university we have departments such as Student Legal Services, Registration and Records, and Financial Aid that have active assessment programs and even measure student-learning outcomes. In reviewing previous ACPA and NASPA conference presentations, we found that these areas are underrepresented. A great resource for research ideas can be found in *A Research and Scholarship Agenda for the Student Affairs Profession* (NASPA Task Force on Research and Scholarship, 2011). The research agenda provides "contemporary research topics, state-of-the-profession research topics, and professional competency research topics" (p. 2) into which student affairs professional can delve.

Keith and Lundberg (2014) suggest considering the following factors when selecting a good presentation topic: (a) your own interests, (b) your audience's needs and interests, and (c) the specific occasion for the presentation and the relevance of your work to the occasion. In other words, if you're not excited about the work you are doing, then your audience certainly won't be. Also, people will be expecting a certain kind of presentation, as we discussed previously, and one that is about the topic that you promised to the review committee and is now printed in the conference's program. Keep your promise.

Writing the Proposal

It is now time to write your program proposal. To do so, you may wish to consider these suggestions from the ACPA 2014 Convention Program Team (ACPA, 2014):

- Provide supporting research and data within the body of the program proposal.
- Apply relevant theory to strengthen your proposal.
- Provide learning outcomes that are clear and concise.
- Avoid unnecessarily large presenting teams.
- Stay within the word limit for all of the fields.
- Include an outline of the session agenda, preferably with time frames for each part.

The structure of your program proposal may vary depending on the type of session you have selected. A program proposal typically includes an abstract, a program title, and a description. The abstract is a brief yet thorough description of your proposal. Essentially, the abstract summarizes your proposal and is often the description used in the conference program. You may have as few as 100 words to capture the essence of your presentation, so get to the point quickly and be sure to include key words that will alert the reader as to the theory or literature that informed your work. What makes a good proposal title is how it captures the essence of your work and entices participants to explore your work further.

The proposal description is a detailed look at your program proposal and should do the following: Describe your program format (e.g., workshop, roundtable); provide an overview of content, including learning outcomes and how they will be achieved, relevant theory, and match to professional standards and conference theme(s); and specify the potential target audiences. If in doubt as to whether your proposal meets the guidelines of the conference you have chosen, have your peers review it to make sure you are on track. When your proposal is ready, make sure to submit it before the deadline. Submission guidelines are typically listed on the conference website. In the appendix at the end of the chapter you will find an example of a proposal we had accepted for the NASPA Assessment & Persistence Conference in 2012.

What Makes a Good Presentation?

We began this chapter with a true story about a not-so-good experience with presenting at a national conference. Were you engaged? Did you find yourself experiencing any emotion? Often, what draws people to a chapter, and also to a conference session, is a story. Student affairs professionals have lots of stories. You may find yourself sharing them regularly with colleagues and perhaps even your family. You tell these stories because they are memorable for some reason; they stick with you. If you want your presentation to stay with your audience long after the conference is over, consider telling a relevant story that drives home the points you are making. If you want to learn more about listening to stories as a research methodology, we suggest you pursue narrative inquiry (see, e.g., Clandinin & Connelly, 2000).

In addition to the ability to relay a point through a story, good speakers have *presence* (Hoff, 1988). They have a sense of purpose and an outward attitude; they are aware of the audience and their environment. We share here the main elements of presentations and how to do them justice. Although your content is vital, it is only one part of your presentation.

Several years ago, the state of Oregon implemented public-speaking standards in K–12 schools. Its grading rubric (Oregon Department of Education, n.d.), which is still used, consists of the following areas: (a) ideas and content, (b) organization, (c) language, and (d) delivery. These present four discrete areas that give focus to each part of an effective presentation. Although the elements of a good presentation work symbiotically, it may be helpful to think of each of these areas as you are practicing your speech. Rather than believing that you're a pretty good or pretty awful presenter, consider specifically how you're doing in each of these areas:

- *Ideas and content:* clarity and focus of topic; development of ideas with supporting details; connections and conclusions
- *Organization:* strength of introduction and conclusion; clarity of organizational structure; placement of details; transitions
- *Language:* originality and impact of language; word choice
- *Delivery:* eye contact; enunciation; pronunciation; rate; volume; tone; inflections; use of nonverbal techniques such as facial expressions, gestures, body movement, and stage presence

Share these items with your colleagues so they can use them as guidelines for feedback. In addition, don't forget to address issues of accessibility for audience members who may have special visual, auditory, or physical needs.

When it comes to introductions, it's important to really think about the content. Often, presenters will state their name and affiliation or a conference volunteer will briefly introduce them. We find it effective for speakers to introduce themselves by briefly stating their perspectives and the assumptions they bring to what is being shared with their audience. For example, the fact that one of us grew up poor with illiterate parents brings a very different bent to how the world, including student services in higher education, is perceived. Sharing a story in this manner is also effective in engaging your audience.

Conference organizers will often want an outline of how you are going to spend your time. Think about how this time will be best utilized to get your point across, not as something to fill. Some people like being talked to for 60 minutes; however, many do not. As you are thinking about how you're going to present, consider what you want your audience to be doing during this time. What would make your presentation most engaging? Conference sessions often involve participants discussing, free writing and then sharing, or some other activity where people can interact with their peers. Many of our colleagues present now with real-time surveys administered via cell phones. However, the point is not to do an activity for activity's sake but to intentionally create varying formats to keep the audience engaged. We are reminded of the rule of thirds when teaching, which is the idea of dividing a class into three distinct sections that create a cohesive whole. For example, you can spend the first third of your presentation in an active discussion, the second third in direct instruction, and the last third in applying the topic discussed to home campuses. Part of the last third should also include an intentional conclusion. How do you want to end your session so your audience will know it's over? What do you want them to leave with and how best will you do that? Avoid the "That's it" often uttered at many an end of sessions.

Visual Aids

When it comes to the use of visual aids, Gregory (1999) advocates doing the following:

- Appeal to as many senses as possible (see hear, taste, smell, touch).
- Practice with your aids.
- Limit the number of aids.
- Make your aids simple and clear.
- Aim for back-row comprehension.
- Don't circulate your aids.
- Explain your aids.
- Choose intentionally the best time to show your aids.
- Don't talk to your aids.

We add that you think about what you're going to do if someone who is visually impaired attends your presentation. Are these people going to get your message without having to actually see the visual aid? The same is true for people who are deaf or hard of hearing. The strategic use of visual aids along with text should further reinforce your content, create more interest in the topic, and increase the audience's understanding of what is being presented.

Use of Technology and Presentation Software

If you elect to use presentation software, remember that the presentation does not replace your paper. You never, ever, want to stand before an audience and read your slides verbatim. Use your slides as an advanced organizer that will lead the audience down the right path. If you are using a computer or any audiovisual equipment, make sure to have a back-up plan. Although it is not highly common for technology to fail, when it does it can be quite disconcerting. By the time you are ready to present, we are confident you will know your material so well that you can stand in front of your audience (or perhaps behind them or moving around the room) and just share.

Practice

Some of you may be excellent impromptu speakers. You may have received accolades for the entertaining, sincere, and touching words you shared at your department's annual meeting or at your sister's wedding. Most of us, however, feel best when we have rehearsed what we're going to say to an audience, even if it's a small number of people. Begin that rehearsal early. Gregory (1999) suggests the following:

- Practice your presentation all the way through at least four times.
- Practice ideas, not words.
- Time yourself.
- Go all the way through your speech without stopping, especially if you mess up.
- Consider practicing in front of a mirror or in front of a live audience, even if it's an audience of one.
- Make a trial run in the room in which you'll be presenting if you can (at least look at the room the day before your presentation, if possible).
- Make sure you practice the beginning and ending.
- Don't put too many words in your notes.

One of our colleagues has a five-point rule, one for each finger. He distills his presentation to five main thoughts, memorizes these, and then uses visual aids or notes to go into more detail. Another colleague uses only key visuals (such as a picture of a mirror to represent the concept of reflection) and simply practices the presentation over and over again.

The Audience

As we stated in the "What Makes a Good Presentation Topic?" section of this chapter, one component of presenting is a promise to your audience that you will deliver what they expect. You can't do that without first knowing your audience. Gregory (1999) says the most common mistake made by speakers is failing to tailor a presentation or speech to the needs and interests of the audience. A good presenter knows what the audience knows or at least has a good idea of what the audience is bringing to the partnership. To "reach your listeners and change them" (Gregory, 1999, p. 63), you must be audience-centered, not a performer or the sage on the stage. This is especially important to keep in mind if you are conducting longer workshops, which can range from a half day to multiple days. Conferences often charge hefty extra fees for these workshops, so participants should get what they paid for: a professional development experience that is targeted specifically to them. As a presenter for a short session or multiday workshop, you owe your audience no less.

ℰℭ

A good presenter knows what the audience knows or at least has a good idea of what the audience is bringing to the partnership.

ℰℭ

Being an audience-centered presenter also means being very aware of the diverse needs of your audience. This encompasses everything from language to accessibility, to the examples you use for context, and much more. Although you will know that people attending your conference session are interested in some topic of education for some reason and are likely to be members of the organization hosting the event, you probably will not know the breadth of their backgrounds or the needs of specific audience members. As a presenter, you cannot make assumptions about your audience, and you need to be adaptable to whoever appears at your session. Are you ready to respond directly to the conference participant who has a hearing impairment, rather than to her sign-language interpreter? Is the presentation that you will upload to the conference site friendly for screen readers? Will the international participant understand the idioms and jargon you are using?

ℰℭ

Being an audience-centered presenter also means being very aware of the diverse needs of your audience. This encompasses everything from language, to accessibility, to the examples you use for context, and much more.

ℰℭ

Think of your presentation as both a teaching and learning opportunity for you and your audience. As a teacher you want to know that you are connecting with your audience and that they understand what you are presenting. After introducing yourself, telling a story perhaps, and sharing what you bring to the session, provide a brief overview of where the presentation is going so that the audience knows what to expect. You might want to take a quick survey by a show of hands to determine which parts of your presentation will be most relevant to your audience and modify your presentation accordingly. Let them know in advance if you welcome questions during your presentation or want to wait until after you are done. While you are presenting, if your audience looks confused, you may need to slow down, take stock of what you are saying, and perhaps even encourage them to ask questions. In much of the Western world, it is expected that you make regular eye contact. Allow time at the end for your audience to ask questions to clarify any misunderstandings, to explore information in more depth, or for you to learn from their perspectives. After presenting, make sure to thank your audience for attending as well as provide information on how attendees can contact you for follow-up information and how they can access handouts from your presentation.

&)C?

Think of your presentation as both a teaching and learning opportunity for you and your audience.

&)C?

After the Presentation

One of the most valuable things you can do to improve your presenting skills is to reflect (remember Dewey in chapter 1). Think about the last time you did something that was evaluated in some way, whether by an audience or in a classroom. Did you wonder what worked and what didn't? What would you have removed or added? Did you really feel like reflecting on your process? Probably not. We encourage you, however, to do just that after your presentation (and after your next evaluation or exam). Hoff (1988) suggests these steps if you are critiquing a presenter, including yourself: (a) find something specific that was good about your presentation, (b) characterize the entire presentation before criticizing yourself as the presenter, and (c) focus the critique toward the future—what specific thing will you do differently or keep the same the next time you present?

To help prompt this reflection, conferences often disseminate evaluations. These evaluations (digitally or in print) ideally are summarized and returned to presenters shortly after they have completed their presentation. Do take these evaluations seriously and use them to help you reflect on what you would like to do the next time you present. Even if the conference has a formal evaluation system, you can plan on saving the last five minutes of your presentation for your own evaluation prompt. Unfortunately, these evaluations that come after the session is over will not help your immediate audience, so we also like the idea of taking a pulse during your session. This formative assessment can be as simple as asking your audience to jot down the two main points about your topic, which will let you know whether your audience truly understood what you were saying, before you continue on with your presentation.

Creating and Presenting Effective Webinars

What if your presentation is not face-to-face but instead is presented in a webinar? All the elements mentioned thus far are important in creating and delivering an effective webinar. In deciding whether a webinar is the best tool for your presentation, consider your audience, the content, and the time needed to cover the material (Peters & Griffiths, 2012). Many webinars are only by invitation and some offer a speaker fee. It is also possible you will be asked to do a webinar as a professional courtesy as part of your membership in an organization. If you are paid to present, more than likely the expectations for the quality of content and delivery will be greater.

Webinars can have many benefits. For example, travel budgets have become more limited in higher education, so being able to conduct a webinar from your office with others located around the world is more cost effective and the potential for outreach is that much greater. Webinars, done well, can be dynamic and entertaining by incorporating audio, video, animation, and stories. Moreover, you can develop your presentation for a target audience and engage them early and often. From the initial invitation to attend the webinar through the postwebinar contact, you will have an opportunity to connect with your target audience and create more engagement. In addition, many webinar software platforms can track who participates and why, and this information can be captured upon registration. You can also collect data during and after the webinar through survey and polling features and chat capture. If you record and archive your presentation, the opportunities to stay connected to participants increase.

What makes a good webinar presentation? An abundance of information that will guide you through this process is available on the Internet. We have condensed the key points from our readings to assist you. For more information about creating and presenting webinars, see Agron (2012), Anderson (2010), Communiqué Conferencing (2003), Fripp (2009), Mitchell (2010), Peters and Griffiths (2012), and Wang and Hsu (2008).

Consider your target audience, the content you want to convey, and the goals of your webinar. Given your goals, what specific objectives do you have for your audience? That is, what do you hope they will learn as a result of your webinar? Structure the content then with these objectives in mind. When you present at a distance, you will not have the visual cues from your audience that they are engaged and understanding your presentation. Engagement is key when presenting to audiences at a distance, and the use of visual aids is essential. In creating your presentation, you will want to use more slides than usual, with the majority of the slides containing little text and more visuals. Consider using graphics and animation to engage the audience and to convey your main points.

In addition to visual aids, consider how you will communicate with your audience. One option might be to pose questions to the audience and encourage feedback. Another might be to allow your audience to pose questions to you during the presentation.

Even given great content and delivery, you will need to test your presentation before you go live. Given the software platform you have selected, you will need to make a few decisions beforehand. Does the platform allow for one-way communication, such as audio streaming, or two-way communication, such as teleconferencing? Does the software have the capability for audience polling, chat, question and answer, and recordings? In addition, webinars are very difficult to deliver alone. Typically you will have to have at least a moderator to introduce you, to field audience questions, and to gauge the level of audience engagement by their comments and questions (Communiqué Conferencing, 2003). Besides the moderator, who will handle any technical issues that might arise? In addition, consider how you will promote your webinar. Will an organization or a company promote you or will you be expected to promote yourself? If so, do you feel comfortable doing that?

Once you feel comfortable that your presentation is informative and engaging, and you've handled the delivery and support elements, it is time to do a trial run to make sure all the parts work together. Select a friend or colleague to be your participant and have your moderator and technology support involved. In your run-through, make sure that all visuals and hyperlinks load appropriately. Use the same computer, webcam, and headset you will use on the day of the presentation. Avoid using a stand-alone mike because this typically produces feedback, or echo effect, when interacting with participants (Anderson, 2010). You will want to time your presentation with the question-and-answer period and appropriate pauses built in. On the day of the presentation, show up early to make sure everything is working.

Before you close your presentation, ask the audience what questions they have. A good moderator will have tracked questions as the presentation was in progress. Any good presentation ends with encouraging the audience to use the information, so challenge or inspire them to do so. Also, be sure to follow up with your audience with any materials you promised, and don't forget to thank them for participating.

Appendix

NASPA Assessment & Persistence Conference Proposal 2012

Program title:	Creating a culture of doing, using, and sharing assessment
Track:	Assessment
Learning track:	Fundamentals of assessment
Program type:	Concurrent session
Content level:	Beginner
Professional competency areas:	Assessment, evaluation, and research
Audiovisual:	LCD projector and screen

Program Abstract (80 words)

Want to know how to create a culture of doing and using assessment? It is not a secret that the most effective assessment programs have similar things in common: strong leadership, clear vision, and infrastructure and resources that support assessment. Find out how Enrollment Management and Student Affairs at Portland State University (PSU) is successfully creating a culture of assessment through their leadership and assessment council.

Background of Presenters/Familiarity of Topic

Presenter 1: Vicki L. Wise, PhD, Director of Assessment & Research, Portland State University
Presenter 2: May Ann Barham, Director of Advising & Career Services, Portland State University
Presenter 3: Lisa Hatfield, Director of the Learning Center, Portland State University

Outline/Description

Overview and Learning Outcomes

In this session, participants will discover strategies and engage in activities that will help them to create their own culture of assessment. Participants will learn how to develop and grow a student affairs (SA) assessment council, to work collaboratively, to provide support to all SA staff with training and resources as they develop their assessment competency, to create standardized assessment planning and annual reporting templates, to increase visibility of assessment in student affairs, to remove as many obstacles to assessment as possible, and to reward excellence.

Relationship of the Program to the Conference Themes

My charge as the new Assessment Director in Enrollment Management and Student Affairs (EMSA) at PSU was to create a culture for data-driven decision making. Sounds enticing and challenging, doesn't it? Creating this culture takes more than developing and implementing an assessment plan; it is a systemic and systematic process that begins with strong leadership and continues by effective use of data. My charge has been to take the vision of our leadership and to put this vision into practice. For this to happen, I knew that I would need champions who support the vision to move assessment forward. To this end, we have formed the Student Affairs Assessment Council (SAAC) consisting of members that represent both Student and Academic Affairs. The copresenters for this session are members of this Council.

The culture we are creating in EMSA at PSU is inspired by and grounded in solid research and theory. Our framework for creating an infrastructure is derived from research by the Student Affairs Leadership Council (2009) and Lakos and Phipps (2004).

Lakos, A., & Phipps, S. E. (2004). Creating a culture of assessment: A catalyst for organizational change. *Portal: Libraries and the Academy, 4*(3), 345–361. doi: 10.1353/pla.2004.0052
Student Affairs Leadership Council. (2009). *The data-driven student affairs enterprise: Strategies and best practices for instilling a culture of accountability.* Washington, DC: The Advisory Board Company.

Identification of the Program Format (e.g., lecture, panel, debate)

We will share the process we used, including examples, tools, and resources. Participants will engage with the tools and each other and consider ways that these tools can be applied to their home institutions. Participants will also have digital access to all information shared.

4

THE PUBLICATION

You may have picked up this book because you are interested in publishing your work. Perhaps you've never submitted a paper for publication or maybe you need to revisit the writing processes you learned about in graduate school, but the idea of seeing your name in print piques your interest. In this chapter, we provide practical steps to guide you through the process of writing for publication. There is a flow and structure to writing for publication, and though the parts may vary slightly depending on whether you are publishing short pieces on the web or creating a journal manuscript, what is consistent is that good writing takes the writer through a journey of discovery.

ℰℭ

Good writing takes the writer through a journey of discovery.

ℰℭ

Many avenues are available for publishing: book reviews, practitioner papers, research papers, books, book chapters, and a variety of online outlets. Before deciding where you want to publish, think about your ideas and the audience with whom they would resonate. Also, could an online posting evolve into a journal article or even a book? If you have written a thesis or dissertation, are there more publishing ideas in that work just waiting to be explored? What are you really passionate about? What sincere questions do you have about your work? Next, think about the amount of time you have to dedicate to the writing and submission processes. Finally, be honest with yourself about your comfort with writing. If you are new to writing for publication, it might be great to start with a practitioner piece for a publication that has a less rigorous review process because there may be a greater likelihood of having your work published.

Blogs, Wikis, and Other Online Media

Blogs are ubiquitous because creating a blog is as easy as opening a WordPress account. If you have the time to update content, and you like interacting with an audience, you might seriously consider keeping up a blog. Notice that we didn't say *writing* a blog. Many a blog has succumbed to the "I-really-want-to-write-what-I'm-passionate-about-but-I-didn't-realize-it-would-take-so-much-time" syndrome. Good writing, digital or otherwise, simply takes a lot of time. If you decide to make the time and have the passion, then maintaining a blog may be an effective way to communicate your ideas and interests to others.

In addition to writing regularly (twice weekly is a good rule of thumb), according to the definitive book *Blogging for Dummies* (Gardner & Birley, 2010), other common characteristics of a well-maintained blog include a chronological ordering of blog posts, an avenue for comments by readers, archives for the frequent updates and thus the unwieldy number of posts, and the ability for readers to sort by categories.

Writing for digital media may seem like an easy alternative to writing a lengthier piece of work, but don't be fooled into thinking this. Writing online content requires conveying your message with brevity. Information provided online must be "conveyed in a provocative, clever, amusing, interesting, or profound way" (Carroll, 2010, p. 24). Also, you will need to get to the point quickly in your writing. Be warned, some of the rules for word length, paragraph length, and sentence structure simply do not apply here. Gould (2013) in her online blog and Barr in *The Yahoo! Style Guide: The Ultimate Sourcebook for Writing, Editing, and Creating Content for the Digital World* (Barr & Yahoo! Inc., 2010) propose these tips for writing online:

- Keep in mind that blog posts are short, typically 300–500 words; e-newsletters run 25–150 words; and website modules are 75–125 words.
- Use words of three or fewer syllables. Choose common words suited for a sixth- to eighth-grade reading-ease level.
- Construct sentences of no more than 14 words. Paragraphs can be as little as one word or one sentence. Keep it simple with only one or two ideas per paragraph.

ℬ℘

Writing for digital media may seem like an easy alternative to writing a lengthier piece of work, but don't be fooled into thinking this.
ℬ℘

Write for the world by making language gender inclusive; avoid location-specific references, specialized terms and jargon, and culture-specific slang or terms. Most of all, make content accessible to those who are visually impaired by adding alternative text to all visuals. By labeling each image with a brief description of what it is, screen readers will be able to voice to readers what they are unable to see in that image. You may also consider recording yourself reading content and uploading the file. Lastly, many education institutions have screen-reading software such as JAWS or VoiceOver. Try running your text through one of these programs to hear how your words come across. Also, use the settings of headings, subheadings, and bulleted text to convey information. Headings, which are automatically larger and boldfaced, and other visual cues will focus the reader's attention. The use of active voice and present tense will keep writing lively and the reader engaged. Avoid extra words when one word will do.

So Many Journals: How Do I Choose?

Do you want to supplement a blog or tackle a journal paper? Look at the research you have read or the scholars you cite in any research you have done. What journals are these scholars publishing in and what journals do you tend to read? Before deciding where to submit your paper, take some time to peruse the myriad student affairs journals. You'll notice that they differ in article formatting, image presentation, and even intended audiences. Spend some time analyzing them even if you've just begun entertaining the idea of writing for publication. As part of your decision making, look at the articles published in a particular journal to determine whether or not the focus of your paper is suitable for the purpose of that journal. Not all journals will be the right fit for your paper; spend the energy now to determine which one will be best. If in doubt, just e-mail the editor with your idea and ask.

After selecting the journal, the next step is to read the submission process guidelines carefully. Most journals have this information online, and many have an online or e-mail submission process. Make sure to pay close attention to requirements regarding length of your paper, style guidelines, and submission instructions. This will save both you and the editor time.

Ethically, you should submit your paper to only one journal at a time, so choose wisely. There are no journal article police, but if you do submit your prose to several journals and then find that more than one has accepted your piece, your professional reputation will suffer.

Dannelle Stevens, a professor in the Graduate School of Education at Portland State University (PSU), has created a schema to help identify potential journals (see Table 4.1). If you are new to writing papers for journals, you may want to consider submitting your piece to what Stevens calls a third-generation journal, which is not necessarily peer reviewed (read further for more discussion about this) and is often practitioner friendly. In other words, these journals share best (or better) practices of what people are doing in their work. This is in contrast to first-generation journals, which are peer reviewed, entail original research, require use of accepted practices of methodology, are formatted in a typical academic manner, and whose main audience are researchers. Lastly, second-generation journals are those that are somewhere in between the other two, often including articles that summarize others' research.

Don't be fooled into thinking that third-generation journals are second rate or not scrutinized. If such a journal accepts your piece, you'll get plenty of feedback from a reviewer or an editor. For those new to publishing, you may want to focus your efforts on these kinds of journals.

Book Reviews

During the 2012–13 school year, Dannelle Stevens and Micki Caskey, the associate dean of PSU's Graduate School of Education, cotaught a doctoral student leadership seminar that focused on developing identities as scholar practitioners. This educational doctoral program, like many in the country, caters to working adults who have very busy lives outside of graduate school. One of the assignments to foster an identity of scholar practitioner and leader required students to submit a book review to a journal. Given that all the students were familiar with books in their doctoral interest areas, and all had written numerous papers over the years, it seemed a fairly simple segue to write a book review and send it off to a publisher "out there" and patiently wait for the verdict. Students, however, felt some trepidation as they journeyed through the process of finding a current book that interested them; selecting a journal that was a right fit; writing in language appropriate for an audience beyond their peers, professors, and office colleagues; and hitting that final "send" button. However, they all did it, and some of the book reviews were even published.

We hope you're saying to yourself, "If students who have full-time jobs, have families, and are full-time doctoral students can write a book review and submit it to a journal, so can I!" Writing a book review is an ideal way to begin getting published: You are most likely going to choose a topic you want to learn more about; the book should be fairly new, so it's not likely many other people will have read it or, more important, reviewed it; and the process isn't nearly as arduous as writing a research paper.

TABLE 4.1.
Generational Research

Generation	Definition	Text Structure Elements	References	Examples of Journals
First	Peer reviewed Qualitative Quantitative Mixed methods	Abstract Detailed title Common research format Pages numbered across issues in one volume (year) Results often numerically represented in tables Audience: researcher	Numerous Used to find other sources	*Journal of Student Affairs Research and Practice* *Journal of College Student Development*
Second	Peer reviewed Qualitative Quantitative Mixed methods	Abstract sometimes Often a review article Often summarizes a series of research Pages numbered across issues in one volume (year) Can be action research Sometimes photos Audience: researcher, informed practitioner	Numerous, especially if a review article	*Review of Educational Research*
Third	Not necessarily peer reviewed Editor or editorial board review	No abstract Can have catchy title Little attention to methods Sidebars Summary of findings Quick read, user friendly Photos, advertisements Audience: informed practitioner	Few Usually no references within text	*Leadership Exchange* *About Campus*

Note. Schema created by Dannelle Stevens. Copyright D. Stevens, April 2002. Used with permission.

How do you begin? Remember those third-generation journals we mentioned? These are the perfect places for book reviews, so start scanning these kinds of journals to see if they even accept them. If they do, they'll say so; if not, but you are unsure, contact the editors. The doctoral students we mentioned found that some online journals took rolling submissions; others talked with editors who wanted the reviews by hard deadlines. Many students were surprised at the length requirements they were given—some seemed too short to write anything worthwhile and others required much more energy than students had anticipated. When given a word count or page length, regardless of its perceived limitations or ampleness, stick to it. One thousand words means 1,000 words, not 1,001. Document length and other style requirements will be in the journal's publishing guidelines. Read these carefully and adhere to them strictly.

You may remember the magic moment sometime during middle school when your English teachers began making comments like these on your writings about class readings: "I've read this book, so I know what happens. Tell me what *you* think about it" or "Don't just summarize the plot. How does this compare with other books we've read recently?" They were making you think (and they were also probably trying to save themselves from having to read 30 papers that sounded the same). The purpose of a book review is to convince others to read or not read the book at hand. Student affairs professionals, as you are acutely aware, often do not have the luxury of time or money, so will this one book help them with their work? Does it add to our knowledge or synthesize existing knowledge in a useful way? If so, in what ways? In addition to critically looking at content, consider the writing style. Do the authors or editors bring in other voices? How is the book organized? Are there gaps in its coverage?

Research Papers

Writing a research manuscript may seem like a daunting task. Most journals receive more manuscripts than they can ever publish, so yours needs to stand out. The less the journal editor and reviewers have to criticize about your paper, the more likely you are to be published. As Paul Silvia (2007) penned in *How to Write a Lot,* "Because no journals have rejection rates below 50%, I assume that each paper I submit will be rejected" (p. 98). We don't want this to stop you, however, so let's explore ways to increase your chances for acceptance.

Research Ideas

Does coming up with research ideas leave you stymied? Consider *A Research and Scholarship Agenda for the Student Affairs Profession,* which was created by the NASPA Task Force on Research and Scholarship (2011) for inspiring ideas about possible paper topics. This document is a great resource for topics related to contemporary research, state-of-the-profession research, as well as professional competency research. Just like writing a book review or blog post, choose an area of research that really interests you, an area that you can stick with through multiple revisions. Selecting an area that relates to your work may be ideal because your practice and research can dovetail and reinforce each other and allow you to be more productive. Moreover, think of your paper as a way to tell your story: What amount of detail do the audience, reviewer, and editors need to have? You will need to provide enough detail so that others can assess the credibility and transferability of your study.

ಐೊಲ

Choose an area of research that really interests you, an area that you can stick with through multiple revisions.

ಐೊಲ

Essential Parts of the Manuscript

According to Silvia (2007), "Writing a journal article is like writing a screenplay for a romantic comedy: You need to learn a formula" (p. 78). There are many great resources available to you, but we suggest that as student affairs scholar practitioners you follow the *Publication Manual of the American Psychological Association* (APA, 2010) style guide. If you switch to law, history, or another discipline, be sure to learn what style is used in those fields. For student affairs journals and typically the social sciences, APA style is "an authoritative source on all aspects of scholarly writing" (p. 3).

Good scholarly writing typically begins with an outline, but it will look different for each writer. Silvia (2007) posits, and we agree, that outlining allows you to get your thoughts together and affords you the opportunity to decide about length, structure, and audience. Based on APA (2010) guidelines, the standard elements of a manuscript include the title, author information, abstract, introduction, method, results, discussion, and references. You may also include footnotes, appendices, figures, and tables, if needed. Be sure to review the journal guidelines.

Title and Author

You will want a descriptive yet not too lengthy title. As Silvia (2007) recommends, "If tempted to write a trendy, topical, or comical title, think about how it will sound in 10 years" (p. 81). On this same page include author names and institutional affiliations.

Abstract

The abstract may be one of the most difficult parts of your paper to write. Abstracts are typically fewer than 250 words, and can be as few as 75 for some journals. In this short paragraph, you will need to provide a concise description of your study. The abstract should include the problem you addressed, how you addressed it and with whom, what you found, and what it means in relation to the problem. Here is a sample title and abstract (Wise, Spiegel, & Bruning, 1999):

> *Using Teacher Reflective Practice to Evaluate Professional Development in Mathematics and Science.* Describes the PEERS (Promoting Educational Excellence Regionally and Statewide) academy, a series of two-week professional development workshops to model best practices in K–12 science and mathematics teaching and to encourage more constructivist teaching approaches. Participants completed program evaluations and a follow-up study involving reflective practice. Results indicated that teachers put PEERS concepts and strategies into practice in their teaching. (p. 42)

Moreover, abstracts "allow for persons interested in the document to retrieve it from abstracting and indexing databases" (APA, 2010, p. 25). The keywords embedded in your abstract will make retrieval much easier.

Introduction

We agree with Silvia (2007) that the introduction should have three sections: (a) an overview of the problem, (b) a review of relevant theories and findings, and (c) how the current study addresses the problem. The overview of the problem places the study in a broader context for the reader by describing the significance of the problem, outside of the immediate study, and why the problem is important to explore. The literature review should not be exhaustive but should include seminal work, where applicable, and should directly relate to the current problem or study. Depending on the audience you are writing for, it is safe to make assumptions about their level of understanding of the issue if it is well documented, so don't rehash old history unnecessarily. You should conclude this section with a transition to the current study and how you plan to address the problem that prompted your research. This is the section in which you will include your research hypotheses if you have them and how they were derived from the literature review.

Method

The main point of the method section is to convey to the reader how carefully you conducted your research, lending credibility to whether the study is replicable or transferable to another similar setting (Silvia, 2007).

Describe for the reader your study's participants, sampling procedures, measures or instruments, and methodological design. How were your site and sample selected? What were your specific data collection procedures? It is here that you will describe any instrumentation used (e.g., survey, test, rubric, interview, or observational protocol) and its psychometric properties, as applicable. For more information about quantitative, qualitative, and mixed-methods design, see Creswell (2003), Denzin and Lincoln (2000), and Tashakkori and Teddlie (2003).

Results

Now it is time to report what you found and how you found it. Describe your data analysis and interpretation procedures. What analyses did you perform that allowed you to address your problem statement and hypotheses? How did you analyze observational or interview data? If you are conducting a qualitative study you will discuss the data analyses within the research strategy used (e.g., biography, phenomenology, grounded theory, ethnography, case study). Include information on any software used to analyze the data. This is also where you report your methods for determining the quality of data. Using tables and figures is a great way to convey your results visually and allow you to touch on relevant findings.

Discussion

Wow, you're almost there, so no time to lose steam. In the discussion section, you need to deliver the conclusions from your research and show how they relate to your original problem. Be sure to share any surprising findings as well as any limitations. This is the place where you put your study in a larger context. Remember, a focus of doing original quantitative research is to allow others either to replicate your study or to generalize your findings to their context. In a qualitative study, you will place the discussion within the research strategy. For example, if you conducted a biographical study, your discussion will include stories, epiphanies, or historical content to convey a detailed picture of an individual's life (Creswell, 1998). By conveying this level of detail, it is then up to the reader to determine whether findings are transferable to his or her own institution.

References

This should not come as earth-shattering news, but make sure that every piece of literature you cite in the paper is also included in the reference section and every reference is cited in the text. Don't cite literature that is not used. As a scholar practitioner, you should always try to find the actual works referenced in articles you have found. In other words, don't use an article referenced by others if you haven't read it yourself. Refer to the APA (2010) style guide for specific instructions on how to cite properly. Also, don't be hesitant to cite your own previous works if you have any that are relevant; this conveys to the editors, reviewers, and readers that you have an invested interest in the topic.

Footnotes, Appendices, Figures, and Tables
Although footnotes, appendices, figures, and tables are not required, we strongly recommend using them if they aid the reader in interpreting your findings. Again, be sure to follow APA standards in doing so.

Submission Process

You have revisited the journal guidelines for submission requirements and are now ready to submit your paper to the journal editor. The journal editor will assign the paper to reviewers using a blind review process, so you will need to eliminate any identifying information, such as author name or affiliation (details about peer review are discussed later in this chapter). Write a letter to the editor and include your contact information; also note that your paper typically needs to be an original piece of work and that has not been submitted elsewhere for publication.

There is one final check we suggest you do before submitting your paper, and that is to review the APA style guide's "Checklist for Manuscript Submission" (APA, 2010, pp. 241–243).

Practitioner Papers

Writing a practitioner-based paper for publication is a great way to share your work experiences, and it certainly can be less intimidating than submitting a paper to a peer-reviewed scholarly journal. Many people think that only original research papers can be published, so they delay pursuing publication because they just don't have the time or energy to think through a research design and conduct the actual research. However, as we shared when we talked about the various generations of journals, writing about what you're doing can also be published. Maxwell (2012) points out how personal experiential knowledge can be valuable in supporting your conceptual framework, or the beliefs and theories that guide your research: "Unfortunately, many students, and other researchers as well, ignore what they know from direct experience, because it isn't seen as being credible or prestigious as 'the literature'" (p. 87). Practitioners appreciate learning about what they can do right now or what has worked at other institutions to address common challenges.

What types of things might you write about? Why not share your program development efforts, observations you have noted after years in the field, a review of the literature, or a how-to guide, to name a few. What about that conference presentation you were just going to put on the shelf? And remember to review *A Research and Scholarship Agenda for the Student Affairs Profession* (NASPA Task Force on Research and Scholarship, 2011) for topics.

You are the one with firsthand experience in your area, so write about issues that you care about and that will have practical relevance for others. Many student affairs organizations offer opportunities for practitioners to contribute to their publications. These organizations and their publications include the following:

- *The Journal of College Orientation and Transition* (National Orientation Directors Association, NODA)
- *Developments* and *Journal of College Student Development* (American College Personnel Association, ACPA)
- *Career Development Quarterly* (National Career Development Association, NCDA)

ℰᏩ

You are the one with firsthand experience in your area, so write about issues that you care about and that will have practical relevance for others.

ℰᏩ

Practitioner papers typically take on a different structure from research papers because the structure is dictated more by the topic than by requirements in the APA checklist. As with all good writing, there is a logic and an organization to the information. The review process may be as stringent as the review for a scholarly journal but may not include a blind review, so it is important to check the publication guidelines (Dilley & Hart, 2009).

Review Process

Peer review is the evaluation of professional writing and research by others working in the same field. Typically when you submit a paper to a publication that has a review process, the reviewers will determine whether the paper addresses a question of importance to its respective field and whether the problem statement is clearly specified. Reviewers will next examine the paper to determine whether the methodology, conventions, and style are sound. They will then make recommendations to the journal's editor as to whether your manuscript should be accepted.

If you have submitted your paper to a peer-reviewed journal in student affairs and are anxiously awaiting editorial feedback, you're not alone. In 2008, a whopping 1.3 million papers were published in peer-reviewed journals (Sense About Science, 2009). Why have a peer review process? Scholarship calls for integrity, originality, and plain old good writing. This process helps maintain these crucial factors—there are no journal-writing police. The bottom line is peer review makes for a better paper. In a survey of more than 4,000 authors and reviewers, an overwhelming majority of researchers (91%) felt their last paper was improved as a result of peer review (Sense About Science, 2009).

Depending on the journal, feedback can result in basically three outcomes. One, the journal editors can love your paper and accept it as is. Two, your paper may be flatly rejected. Or three, your piece may come back as a revise and resubmit, meaning the journal editors will consider your paper if you make the suggested changes. You will need to address every point in the reviewers' comments and make the appropriate changes. If in doubt as to what is suggested, seek clarification from the editor or from a colleague who has experience with publishing. There are times when you won't agree with reviewers' suggestions. In such a case, if you have substantial justification for not making recommended changes, be sure to note this when you resubmit your revised paper. There are no guarantees that your paper will be published when you resubmit it, but by making your paper stronger you can then submit it to another publication if rejected from the first. It is important to note that publications vary in their turnaround time, so make sure to check submission requirements on the publication website. When in doubt, it is wholly appropriate to contact the editor to inquire about timelines.

Belcher (2009) suggests that you read an editor's response during a time when you can emotionally absorb a publication decision. It may be hard to resist opening that e-mail between calls or meetings so go ahead, but then go back to it when you have intentionally set aside a good chunk of time to process the feedback. Even if your paper is accepted, you will need time to digest the critical comments. Will you choose to throw away your submission because you can't take the criticism? Will you be professional or accusatory in your correspondence with the editor? Will you earnestly try to address the reviewers' comments?

Of course, the least favorable outcome is a flat-out rejection of your paper. "If you write, you will be rejected. This is unavoidable," says Belcher (2009). "The important thing is not to let it stop you" (p. 8). Press on and take time to read the reviewers' comments because it may still be possible to redo the paper and submit it elsewhere in another form. For example, it may be that your paper in a much shorter version would be perfect for an online publication that is not peer reviewed. Even if you don't submit it elsewhere, learn from the rejection; it is only one part of your journey as a writer. How you handle a rejection may determine your next steps in your scholarly journey.

Final Note: Can I Add This to My CV?

A curriculum vitae, or CV, is a document of your life's professional work. In the United States, scholar practitioners should keep up-to-date CVs instead of résumés because CVs go into much more detail of what you have done. Subheadings of CVs include relevant experiences, publications, presentations, grants, and awards. Writings that have been published or that have been submitted for publication should be included in your CV. Even unpublished research or manuscripts can be included.

You should list the blog you manage on your CV; however, some editors may not value blog writings as much as pieces published in journals. With technology—and the writing and dissemination associated with it—changing daily, editors may soon have to consider such work as published material. However, for now, the peer review process remains the standard. We have seen some CVs that have a category such as "Other Creative Endeavors" or "Other Writings" that would fit a blog nicely. Examples of CVs can be found at one of our favorite writing sites, the Purdue Online Writing Lab (https://owl.english.purdue.edu/owl).

5

STRATEGIES FOR STAYING
WITH WRITING

W e're sure that you've never said any of the following: "I don't have time to write"; "I don't have time to read"; "I'll save my writing [or reading or thinking] about complex stuff for Friday." If you can honestly say these thoughts have never entered your mind, well, we look forward to seeing you at the next big conference or to reading your next illuminating article. If you admit uttering one of these phrases, you are not alone. The two of us say these things all the time. The key, though, is we know how to counter these woeful excuses.

Think about it: If you write one page a day, *one* page, you will have written 365 pages in one year. That's a book! For those of you who struggle with writing daily, we are confident that you can produce *one* page of writing in one day. Just think of all the e-mails and text messages you send in a day. Surely, the number of words written add up to at least one page, so we know it's possible. For those of you who are prolific writers (either professionally or personally), we invite you to share your strategies with us and with your colleagues. We both enjoy writing and yet know that sometimes it's just plain tough to do. We advocate the words of Boyle Single (2010): "Fluent writers write regularly, whether they like it or not" (p. 129).

ℰℛℭℛ

*Think about it: If you write one page a day, one page, you
will have written 365 pages in one year.*

ℰℛℭℛ

You may be thinking to yourself that you simply do not have the time to write. If you did, you would have submitted that proposal or kept up the blog you started last year. Instead of the fallback "I don't have any time to [insert

47

activity of choice here]," try very hard to remember to say instead, "I choose to prioritize [insert another preference here] instead." Repeat these sentences to yourself, and you should hear a difference. The latter creates agency. This means that *you* must decide that writing takes priority over something else. You can't do everything, and the sooner you come to grips with this fact, the easier it will be to write.

You may be thinking to yourself that this advice is coming from a couple of student affairs folks who have ample time on their hands. After all, we're writing a book about this. However, we both know quite a bit about not having a lot of time to write. We both work full-time outside the home, serve on many committees, work on journal submissions and conference presentations, have children and pets, and take care of older parents to some extent. One of us is concurrently in a full-time doctoral program. We get the time issue. How do we "find the time" to write? We hold strong the mindset to produce words on paper on a regular basis (remember Carol Dweck's work in chapter 2?). This is a priority for us. It means that we choose to use our time to write and forgo other things that also are important to us. In the future, we will undoubtedly prioritize other important activities but, for now, this is what we are choosing to do.

გOცშ

We choose to use our time to write and forgo other things
that also are important to us.

გOცშ

Dealing With Digital Distractions

What would any of us do without technology? We can share our work from practically anywhere on the planet and chat in real time with people thousands of miles away via our computers and phones. Finding articles to support our research is instantaneous. All this may not seem so amazing to younger folks, but we both remember the days of index cards and carbon copies. While we appreciate the wonders of technology, we also acknowledge that it can all be terribly distracting. How many of our students write papers while on Facebook and Google Hangouts? How many of us can remember the last day we didn't log on or in to something?

If you acknowledge that this may be a problem for you, we encourage you to set a timer for 30 minutes to write with nothing open except your word-processing document. Do this first thing when you get up or right when you get into the office, before life and work pile up on you. Yes, that means even before checking your e-mail. If writing for half an hour without such distractions is problematic, you may want to look into, ironically, electronic help with your digital addiction. One suggestion is LeechBlock (n.d.), which touts itself as a "simple productivity tool designed to block those time-wasting sites that can suck the life out of your working day." Another program is Nanny for Google Chrome (n.d.), which lets you block websites for certain periods of time. To get around the ease of changing options, you can have a colleague (a member of your writing group perhaps) create the password so you aren't even tempted to change the settings.

Adapting to Your Writing Environment

We have colleagues who have very special places in which to write. These vary from weathered desks in an old attic to a garden house built especially for such creative work. Unfortunately, most of us don't have the luxury of such special places. If you have such a space, we envy you. However, though physical environment can be extremely important in making you feel good, don't let it hinder you in your writing. True, you may feel more inclined to write if you have a room of your own, but don't let the perception that you *need* your own special place to write hold you back.

Remember the children and pets we mentioned earlier? They are relevant to our physical writing space as well. One of us writes at the dining room table; the room itself is shared with two guinea pigs in a fairly huge and quite luxurious homemade cage and the art/crafts/homework accoutrements of a first grader. Needless to say, it's not an ideal environment. The laptop, notes, APA stylebook, and anything else are splayed across the table, and when it's time to cook dinner, they all go back in the satchel to rest until the next few moments of production. Silvia (2007) states that "unproductive writers often bemoan the lack of 'their own space' to write. I'm not sympathetic to this creaky excuse" (p. 20). We're not either. Silvia recalls writing in the bathroom. Beat that.

If you are lucky enough to have a smidgen of space you can call your own, do make it comfortable and efficient. Keep a copy of APA or other appropriate style guide nearby, along with any other notes, journals, and guides that you think will be helpful. Add good lighting or, better yet, natural light. The basement might be solitary but is it warm enough? If you need a space heater to keep your writing fingers warm, that shared dining room table might not seem so bad.

Creating an Organized System

After figuring out your space to write, in whatever way that works for you to be productive, you should also create a strategy that will help you stay organized and on track with your writing. There are a number of ways you can do this. For us, it helped to create an online central repository where we shared a writing schedule, chapters we were working on, and research articles. The added benefit of an online system is that we could access our work from anywhere.

Another help that came with the wonders of technology is electronic citation management systems. Mendeley and Zotero are a couple, but there are others out there. These handy applications serve as repositories for PDFs of journal articles and notes as well as simple ways to create and note citations in the right format for your work. They can be synced to your smartphone, desktop, and the cloud. As people who remember writing citations on index cards, we believe these systems are pretty amazing. They also allow you to organize your articles in folders and thus serve as excellent organization tools for the literature you gather. If you are not familiar with citation management systems, ask your institution's librarian for assistance.

Engaging in Collaborations

We have benefited greatly by our collaboration in writing this book. If you feel overwhelmed by the idea of writing alone, then consider forming a partnership with someone who can bring a skill set to both complement and challenge yours. As practitioners in student affairs, we know how programs run, we understand the content and delivery of services, but we may lack specific expertise in research methods or in data analysis and interpretation. Find a partner who has these skill sets and write together. In doing so, each of you will expand your expertise. A good collaborator will help you stick to your timeline and goals as well. The same applies later once you have a draft; you can solicit feedback from those who can give you constructive feedback.

ℰℭ

If you feel overwhelmed by the idea of writing alone, then consider forming a partnership with someone who can bring a skill set to both complement and challenge yours.

ℰℭ

Participating in Writing Groups and Creating Support Systems

Throughout the year of writing this book, we met almost weekly. These meetings lasted anywhere from 30 minutes to two hours, depending on what we wanted to get done. We left each meeting with a goal (read further for more on goal setting) to be met before we got together again. We also were linked electronically through Dropbox. Without this regular support, we doubt you would be reading this text right now.

Dannelle Stevens, who developed the schema of journals we shared in chapter 4, also has created a campuswide writing group for faculty. Called Jump Start, the program is in partnership with Portland State University's Office of Academic Innovation and offers monthly group meetings to discuss strategies for being productive writers. The key element is that each participant is also part of a small writing group of three or four colleagues. These smaller groups meet weekly for an hour and either share their writing updates or use the time to write. These groups serve as a source of accountability as well as a sounding board. Because scheduling can be difficult, some groups meet online during this hour. Although targeted to faculty, the program is open also to student affairs professionals, and a few do participate. We encourage you to seek out any organized writing program on your campus. If there isn't one, start your own with a few colleagues who are motivated like you. Set your hour to meet and remain accountable to each other. And when one of you does get a proposal or paper accepted, remember to celebrate these worthy accomplishments. We talk more about how to create your own groups in chapter 7.

Our institution also occasionally offers writing retreats for faculty. If your institution does so as well, take advantage of them. These are weeklong and are typically held in a building on the edge of campus. If you feel that only faculty should attend, then ask the organizers if staff can also participate. We bet they'll welcome you in.

Setting Goals

Set specified dates for meeting your goals, and then determine how much you need to write per day to reach them. Consider other obligations you may have and set goals that are realistic and within your control. Solicit the support of others in reaching your goals. If you have a collaborative partner, hold each other accountable for timelines and check in with each other on a regular basis. Share your goals with coworkers, family, and friends (anyone who can offer support) and ask them to help. Remember, you aren't going to wait for inspiration; you will write daily to form a habit of writing.

ଘଓ୯ଧ

Consider other obligations you may have and set goals that are realistic and within your control.

ଘଓ୯ଧ

What will you do in those 10 minutes or during one session that you set aside for scholarship? What do you want to get done by next week or next month? If you don't set some sort of goal, you may find yourself wondering just what you did get done. When we work with students at our university, we often raise the concept of SMART goal setting. SMART is an acronym for specific, measurable, attainable, relevant, and time-bound and is often attributed to Peter Drucker's management by objectives concept ("SMART criteria," n.d.). Rather than broad goals such as "I want to be a great writer" or "I want to live a healthy lifestyle," SMART goals can be measured both in criteria for obtaining the goal and in time. For example, your SMART goal may be that you will write for 15 minutes every day this week. In addition to being measurable and time bound, it is relevant to your professional identity and feelings of self-efficacy, and it also is attainable. Some of our colleagues have set SMART goals of writing a certain number of words every day or writing an abstract for presentation submission during one writing session. Silvia (2007) keeps track of the words he has produced in an SPSS file. "The system sounds nerdy, obsessive, and weird, but it helps me stay focused," he claims (p. 40).

If you really think you can't do much in 15 or 30 minutes, try one of the following SMART goals the next time you write:

- Write 100 words without worrying about organization or editing— just get some words and thoughts on paper.
- Copyedit one page of text.
- Note on your calendar what days you'd like to be done with a specified number of tasks.
- Download two articles that may help you with your proposal or paper.
- Find a conference to which you'd like to submit a proposal.
- E-mail someone to interview for your research.
- Check five citations for correct style.
- Walk down the hall and ask your colleague if he or she is willing to read your paper and give feedback.

When your time is up, write down the goal for your next writing session. This way, you have an idea of what you want to do next before you even begin the task.

In addition to setting specific goals for each writing session or time period, we suggest another strategy that we often use with students: Work backward in terms of time. If the conference proposal is due in four weeks, when do you want it done? The deadline might be the obvious answer, but most writing needs to sit for a bit. Choose *your* deadline and then ask yourself, What do I want done three weeks before the deadline? Two weeks? What can I get done in the next three days?

Writing a Little at a Time

In addition to writing regularly, which creates habit, undertake your writing in small chunks. We have colleagues who set timers for 20 or 30 minutes when they get to work (this is before they check e-mail) so they can write. We know people who rise a half hour earlier because once the children are up their focus has to be on getting them ready for school. Are you a night owl? Write for 15 minutes after everyone else in the house has gone to bed. Boice (1990) states that writing in short, daily stints rather than bingeing will help ensure regular productivity.

If you don't believe you can get much done in such short periods of time, think of all the things you can get done in your house in only 10 minutes. You can clean your toilets, iron several articles of clothing, make at least two beds, and even make your lunch to take to work. We'd say that if you've done any of these things today you probably felt pretty productive. Also think about brief time stealers, those minutes when you could be writing a little bit here and there, which add up quickly. Could you watch 30 minutes less of television or check Facebook only once a day? You'd be surprised if you added up all those wasted minutes surfing the Internet in only one day. Consider times that could serve a dual purpose as well. If you use public transportation, could you check a few citations during your commute?

The truth is you can do a lot to move your writing along. We share this because many people believe erroneously that they need several hours in order to write. When was the last time you had several hours to do whatever you wanted? And, really, if you truly did find yourself in this situation, did you get done what you had intended? We hear students across campus saying that they have all weekend to study. We bet if you asked them Sunday night what they had accomplished, many would not be able to tell you.

Inspiring Yourself

Along with the notion that all you need is a lot of time, many people feel they need to be inspired (by what or by whom, we don't know) to write. And once they are inspired, they will surely produce reams of pages. Has this ever truly happened? We encourage you to inspire yourself a little every day. Write for 10 minutes and see how you feel. We bet you'll feel better and perhaps inspired to write a little more. "Start writing before you may feel you're ready," says Boice (1990, p. 86). He also adds that you can even finish writing before you feel you are done. If you write even when you aren't inspired, you create the habit of writing. So, just write and don't worry about how good it is. In the revision phase you will have ample time to make it perfect enough.

6

A BRIEF GUIDE TO STYLE

If you are reading this book, you've most likely written a few papers in your day. Through all the essays, research papers, theses, and even dissertations, have you given much thought to the process of your own writing? Do you write one draft and call it good? Do you spill everything at once without stopping? Do you stare at the screen waiting indeterminately for the perfect word so you can begin your prose? And then what do you do? Writing is not only about putting words on a page or computer screen; the writing process encompasses multiple drafts, revisions, pauses, reflections, edits, pauses again, drafts again, and revisions again, before ultimately calling it not perfect but, rather, good enough.

According to Zinsser (2006), "This fixation on the finished article causes writers a lot of trouble, deflecting them from all the earlier decisions that have to be made to determine its shape and voice and content. It's a very American kind of trouble. We are a culture that worships the winning result" (p. 22). We lose the learning that happens during this process if all we care about is the product that we ultimately submit to an editor. As you begin or continue your writing, pause and reflect on your process. What have you learned? How is that going to help you as you continue down this path of scholarship?

℘◌ℭ

As you begin or continue your writing, pause and reflect
on your process.

℘◌ℭ

Finding Your Voice

If you are new to the writing process you may not yet have found your voice. Clark (2006) says that "voice is an effect created by the writer that reaches the reader through his ears, even when he is receiving the message through his eyes" ("Tool 23: Tune Your Voice," para. 3). But, you ask, how do I find my own voice? To be a good writer, you need to read the work of others. Read fiction and nonfiction (any genre, in fact) and take notes on what you have read. What about the content, word use, and flow captured your interest? We have found that the more we read, the better we write. Plus, the added benefit is that as we read research and take notes about what further questions we have, we create new ideas for future research.

ഇരന

To be a good writer, you need to read the work of others.

ഇരന

Writing a Mission Statement

Consider writing a mission or problem statement about what you hope to accomplish by writing a particular piece. What is it that prompted you to write on this topic? Perhaps you read a research article and in your note taking you wrote questions that needed further exploration. That is a great place to start. Remember, writing starts with your thoughts and ideas. Perhaps you are in the car driving to work reflecting on something you observed in one of your programs. You ponder why things occurred as they did. When you get to work, jot down your questions and read what others have observed. This can truly be the basis for your paper and the beginning of creating an outline. Once you have a sense of the premise of your paper and the questions you hope to answer, you can start to put a structure in place for writing.

ഇരന

Writing starts with your thoughts and ideas.

ഇരന

Knowing Your Audience

At this point, we ask that you consider your intended audience. You want to communicate clearly to the reader, but first you need to know who your reader is. The requirements of the editor are your first priority. As mentioned in chapter 4, review publication guidelines to determine writing requirements. Ask yourself who are the likely readers of your paper and keep them in mind as you write. Don't make assumptions about the readers' levels of knowledge about the topic.

Outlines

Outlines, of some type, serve as road maps of where you want your writing to go; the evidence is consistent that outlining benefits writing (Torrance & Galbraith, 2006). From your mission statement to conclusion, it is on you to guide the reader through your story. It is not unlike planning a road trip. You know where you want to go and when you want to arrive, but you just need to map out the route that will get you there. What topics do you need to cover to address your questions? List all topics that come to mind and prioritize the ones most likely to answer your questions. Go ahead and insert relevant quotes and references to the research of others. You now have a structure in place for writing. You can also try drawing your outline. These concept maps or mind maps are often used as starting points for idea generation, but they are also effective visual organizers because you can see connections between ideas that make sense. You may think that you write best when words just spew forth, and that does indeed work for some people; however, when you get to writing of any sizeable length, especially when references are involved, an outline is one road map that will serve you well.

Outlines serve as organizers, and we particularly like the suggestions offered by Machi and McEvoy (2012) when creating outlines:

- Resist the urge to create a list of facts and ideas. Outlines may help with placing chunks of writing on various topics, but they do not help with transitions.
- Don't include too much information on an outline, which may obscure the bigger picture.
- Include enough detail so that you'll remember what you want to say.

One method for checking organization is to create a reverse outline. After you have written a draft, return to your paper and note what each paragraph is about. Do you have topics of paragraphs (or perhaps even sections) that are talked about in various places? Is there one solitary paragraph about an important variable in your argument? Rereading your draft with organization solely in mind through this reverse outline will only help your writing.

Drafts and "Re-visions"

Writing for publication often means writing several drafts. In fact, you might write so many drafts that you'll actually tire of your topic even though you were once so passionate about it. Don't worry, the passion will return, but don't be surprised if you feel the need to just be done with your paper.

Your first draft will not be perfect (no draft ever is). As we've said, you will write several drafts, so free yourself from the need to get it right the first, second, or even third time. With each draft, you will improve the sentence structure, word choice, and organization. Keep the momentum going and don't get hung up too early. Drafts, including the one that gets published, should be good enough, not award-winning material. It may be helpful to view your drafts not simply as revisions but as *re-visions*. Try to resee, literally, your text. What would someone not familiar with student affairs have to say about your work? What questions would the subject of your research have about your article? "Rewriting is the essence of writing well: it's where the game is won or lost. The idea is hard to accept," states Zinsser (2006). "Most writers don't initially say what they want to say, or say it as well as they could" (p. 83).

ෂ)ඍ

You will write several drafts, so free yourself from the need to get it right the first, second, or even third time.

ෂ)ඍ

We dedicated a brief chapter to feedback early on because we wanted readers to feel more comfortable with receiving comments about their writing. To foster more productive revisions, we encourage you to ask your colleagues for feedback. If you've taken a writing course, you may recall meeting individually with your instructor for a conference or perhaps working with a small group to receive feedback. These writing conferences and writing workshops can also be useful strategies for conference proposals and writing for publication.

Lastly, we want to point out that revising (reseeing) is not the same as copyediting. Copyediting happens after you've addressed questions of content and organization and typically addresses mechanics and spelling. You can craft the most technically correct article with masterful uses of gerunds and past perfect tense and still leave your readers wondering what in the world you are talking about. We've heard many anecdotes from people who have experience with writing centers that students, for the most part, want papers to be edited. In reality, they need help with lots of other things besides commas and parallel construction. Although it is important to know the rules and conventions, remember that revising is not editing.

Writing Structure

Every English teacher should take a general course in linguistics because when we think of writing (and English teachers) we often think of rules. As a former

English teacher, one of us experienced an aha moment when doing exactly this. These rules cover everything from not splitting infinitives to never ending a sentence with a preposition (which we're told someone liked because that's how Latin works; neither of us speaks Latin, so we'll have to trust our sources). Linguists would tell you that language changes and that people once upon a time a long time ago created these rules. In fact, they may have not had much reason to create these "rules." Linguists acknowledge the prescriptive grammar taught in schools, but they also acknowledge the descriptive grammar that happens in everyday language. By grammar, we mean the rules of punctuation, how words function in a sentence, spelling, and all those other conventions that we commonly know as "standard" English. We won't go into the trove of literature about the politics and power of what the term *standard* means here, but we do assume that you want to write for academic publications. This means you'll have to be very familiar with the finer points of academically "standard" English. It may be helpful to use the term *conventions* rather than the term *grammar* because the former suggests these rules are changeable and situated in time and place. If you don't believe that, compare journals published in the United States with those in the United Kingdom.

Our focus is on the prescriptive conventions of writing for academic journals today. Several publications and websites exist that give more information than anyone may want to read about the topic. We therefore offer a few suggestions that address questions students and colleagues have asked regularly about writing for publication. If there is one golden rule for any kind of writing, something to keep in mind always, it is this one by Zinsser (2006): "Simplify, simplify" (p. 16). In other words, cut out the clutter. Zinsser goes on to say, "Few people realize how badly they write. Nobody has shown them how much excess or murkiness has crept into their style and how it obstructs what they are trying to say. . . . The point is you have to strip your writing down before you can build it back up" (pp. 17–18).

Once you've taken away the stuff that has been suffocating your writing, keep these suggestions in mind while bringing it back to what you really want to say:

- *Limit jargon and avoid clichés.* Jargon does not have to be avoided at all cost. There are times when jargon is part of the language of the culture and fits the context, so it works. In higher education, we use a lot of jargon when speaking to coworkers; this is appropriate and makes sense. When presenting or publishing you really need to know your audience, first and foremost, to decide whether a little jargon will work. This can still be risky, so we suggest that to be safe consider your audience lay readers and translate jargon into English that works for those who may not have your expertise. Clichés, on the other hand, should be avoided. These are typically overused phrases, usually involve hackneyed expressions, and often are just poor English usage. Awesome, right?

- *Use active over passive voice.* Active voice demonstrates ownership; we know who is doing the action. Passive voice, on the other hand, tells us who is receiving the action. The problems typically associated with passive voice are that the sentence has more words than it needs, and we are not always sure of the subject-verb-object agreement, which can leave us wondering what a sentence means. Even the current edition of the *Publication Manual of the American Psychological Association* (APA, 2010) reinforces the use of active over passive voice (p. 77).

- *Use personal pronouns correctly.* The requirements of your editors and your ability to tell your story effectively will dictate how you use personal pronouns such as *I, we, us,* and *them.* There are still some scholarly publications for which editors require works in the third person, so check the editorial guidelines. There are times when the use of first person creates an intimacy, a stronger connection with the reader that takes research from a more objective experience to that of a lived experience. It also helps the reader visualize the context and cast of characters more easily.

- *Thoughtfully consider word choice and terminology.* All word usage is relative, and so-called correct usage can vary even within a word (Zinsser, 2006). However, if you go back to your audience, you'll most likely have a better idea of what words to use when as well as when you'll need to elaborate on their meanings. Writing for publication does not mean that you use the longest or rarest words you find simply because you can. You're not trying to impress your reader; instead, you are inviting your audience to read what you have to say because what you have to say is important. The last thing you want to do is alienate your audience. You can assume that you will have some sense of shared vocabulary; however, you may need to define some of the terms you use. You may think you understand what a *midlevel student affairs professional* is because perhaps you are living that role, but have you ever tried to apply a definition to it? If you haven't, you may want to see how ACPA and NASPA define this term.

- *Reduce bias in language.* From the perspectives of many ontological frameworks, there is no objective truth so bias will always exist. Given this, what we can do as writers is to be very aware of the biases that we do own and address these in our writing. In other words, do we call the letter carrier a mailman or the firefighter a fireman without knowing the gender of either? Do we use "people-first" (APA, 2010, p. 76) language such as "person who has a visual impairment"?

- *Effectively use transitions.* You want to make your ideas easy for the reader to follow. To do so, you'll need effective transitions. APA (2010) suggests transitional words that fall under the categories of time links (*then, next, since*), cause-and-effect links (*therefore, as a result*), addition links (*moreover, furthermore*), and contrast links (*but, however, conversely*). These are cues to the reader that change is about to happen. Use your transitions and give your reader the courtesy of a visual and verbal warning. In addition to transitions between paragraphs, you will need to think about transitions between sections of your writing. Journals have varying requirements, so check publication guidelines for help with this. Style guides such as APA will also dictate how sections are separated.
- *Check for appropriate paragraph length.* While we're talking about transitions, you should keep an eye on your paragraph lengths. One paragraph should contain a main idea with supporting details. Should you find your paragraphs looking more like William Faulkner's fiction, then you should step back and see if you truly have just one idea or more of a stream of consciousness. Find the point where the main idea changes, craft a transition, and move on.
- *Use quotes judiciously.* Direct quotations serve a useful role in your writing. They add support to your points, and they bring in other people's voices. However, the writing you are producing should be just that—your own writing. Ballenger (2004) gives a nice guideline: no more than 10% to 20% of your writing should be direct quotes. How do you choose which quotes to insert? Only when you can't say it better yourself. Does the author you are citing say something in a particularly elegant way? If not, it may be better to paraphrase. And don't just plop a quote in your paper without some sort of explanation as to how it fits into your argument. Your manuscript is not a Twitter feed. If you don't know when to indent or where the citations go for your quotes, peruse the appropriate stylebook.

If you want to write better, you should have a handful of books about writing nearby. There are many books on this topic that we could list, but the following few are keepers:

- Graff, G., & Birkenstein, C. (2006). *They say/I say: Moves that matter in academic writing.* New York, NY: W. W. Norton.
  This gem gives excellent practical strategies for improving rhetorical strategies in academic writing. It teaches you, literally, the writing moves that help move the argument and thus the reader to a better understanding of what you are trying to say.

- O'Connor, P. T. (2003). *Woe is I: The grammarphobe's guide to better English in plain English* (Rev. ed.). New York, NY: Riverhead Books.
  Technically, your English teacher may tell you that "woe is I" is correct (look up linking verbs and subject pronouns), but, as O'Connor writes in her humorous book, "The expression 'Woe is me' has been good English for generations. Only a pompous twit—or an author trying to make a point—would use 'I' instead of 'me' here" (p. viii). You'll enjoy the easily readable chapters such as "Comma Sutra" and "Death Sentence."
- Strunk, W., & White, E. B. (1979). *The elements of style* (3rd ed.). New York, NY: MacMillan.
  This "little book" has been on the desks of many a writer. Don't know if you need a comma if you're joining two independent clauses? Don't know what an independent clause is? Then, get a copy of this book, which aims to help the "bewildered reader" who is "in serious trouble most of the time" due to bad writing (p. xvi).
- Truss, L. (2006). *Eats, shoots & leaves: The zero tolerance approach to punctuation.* New York, NY: Gotham Books.
  You've probably heard the joke about the panda that walks into the bar. . . . Read this one if you haven't. And don't forget the children's version, which is a picture book that can benefit people of all ages who remain perplexed by that little comma.
- Zinsser, W. (2006). *On writing well: The classic guide to writing nonfiction* (7th ed.). New York, NY: Collins.
  Contrary to what we've said about audience, Zinsser writes that you are always writing for yourself. "Don't try to visualize the great mass audience. There is no such audience—every reader is a different person" (p. 24). All right, so Zinsser's book has sold more than a million copies and is in its seventh printing. He has a point. Writing, even for publication, is a personal process, both for you as the writer and for each individual reader. As a result, you'll want to have clarity, unity, and the sound of your voice, all of which Zinsser addresses.

Getting Stuck

Okay, there are days you just do not feel like writing. You do not feel inspired, you feel stuck, and the words just won't come. You can still make progress by trying a few simple strategies. If you are sitting in front of a computer screen and the words won't come, then get up and grab a notepad and try writing freehand. Try even moving to another location that might open up ideas.

The simple act of stepping outside with notepad in hand can offer up a new perspective.

Of course, if fear of rejection keeps you from writing, you might try reframing your thinking. Does it help to know that even famous writers have faced rejection on their first books? Stephen King's first book was rejected 30 times before he sold it (Bocco, 2012). Remember, your work won't get published unless you finish it. The worst that can happen is that an editor will reject your paper, which simply means you'll submit it somewhere else, so keep writing.

Style Formats

APA, CMS, and MLA are three main writing styles, which differ mainly in their documentation of sources:

- APA (*Publication Manual of the American Psychological Association*, 2010) is used in psychology, education, and other social sciences.
- MLA (Modern Language Association; *MLA Handbook for Writers of Research Papers*, 2009, and *MLA Style Manual and Guide to Scholarly Publishing*, 2008) is used in English and the humanities.
- CMS (*The Chicago Manual of Style*, 2010) is used in history and some humanities.

Make sure to check with the editorial guidelines for the journal for which you are submitting a paper to verify the most appropriate style to use. The Online Writing Lab (OWL) at Purdue University offers great online resources for each of these styles, as do their respective websites and manuals:

OWL: https://owl.english.purdue.edu/owl/resource/949/01
MLA: www.mla.org
APA: www.apastyle.org
CMS: www.chicagomanualofstyle.org/home.html

7

SCHOLARSHIP SUPPORT GROUPS

You have the motivation and interest to pursue a presentation or publication. If you want to tackle this yourself, you *can* go it solo, and the preceding chapters will help you do this. However, in this chapter we offer tips on working with others to pursue your goals in what we call *scholarship support groups*. Perhaps the most important reason to work with another person or with a group is a simple one: It's more fun. You get to know others better and learn about their families or pets or wild ambitions. You have immediate collective empathy. And even though there can be moments when you'll be frustrated with your work, you can have a good time as well. Working with others gives you perspective on your own work even if your topics of interest have nothing to do with each other. In fact, your group may be more effective if the people in it have different areas of interest because members won't focus on a single topic. In all groups, regardless of size, you can provide a great deal of support just by listening to others' concerns about their work. And they will do likewise.

ജ∝

Perhaps the most important reason to work with another person or with a group is a simple one—it's more fun.

Working with others gives you perspective on your own work even if your topics of interest have nothing to do with each other.

ജ∝

Presenting as a Group

A less intimidating leap into conference presentations is to do so as a duo or small group. If you and a colleague have worked on a project together, this is a natural group for presenting. If you want to create something from scratch, choose your group members wisely (read on for more thoughts about group selection). Limit your group to two to four people; otherwise, scheduling will become a hassle, and each person will not have the opportunity to say very much. Regardless of how many people are in your group, you will want to create your presentation together and then practice together to determine who says what and in what order. Also, if someone can't present, then the other members can easily fill in because they are familiar with the material. We're reminded of a time when we were in a group of three to present and then two members were not able to travel. Needless to say, knowing all the presentation material was very helpful for the one person who did get to present.

As with group publications, you and your group members will have to decide in which order you would like your names to appear in a conference program. Typically, the first person is the one who made more significant contributions such as creating the work itself or having the idea in the first place. Of course, just as with many things in higher education, politics can also play into who gets the first and starring role. If your vice president would rather be first on the list, then perhaps you should let him, even if you think otherwise.

Writing Support Groups

The rest of this chapter is dedicated to writing groups. These models can be modified to fit presenting as well; however, we have found that presentation groups typically converge because members are working together to create one presentation. Writing groups, on the other hand, usually involve individuals working on separate projects. However, they come together for support, accountability, and to learn strategies to move them forward. According to Lee and Boud (2003), writing groups can function to "demystify the process of scholarly writing for publication, to build skills of review and critique, to provide early audiences for draft texts, and so on" (p. 190). Consider some of the following factors in establishing support groups.

Determining Group Size

How many people should be in a supportive group whose goal is to produce scholarship? The answer is simple: It depends. Different numbers of people provide advantages and disadvantages:

- *Two people.* We have worked as a natural pair while writing this book, and that has worked out well for our purpose. It was easy for us to find a weekly common time because only two calendars were involved. However, we sought feedback from others not part of our dyad because we wanted more voices to comment on our work, and we thought it was critical that our work be seen from other perspectives. Unfortunately, if one person can't make a group meeting, you then don't have a meeting. Too many of these and you lose momentum.

- *Three to four people.* The great advantage to this number is more depth in feedback. You also get to know two or three other colleagues well. Although scheduling can be a bit tricky, finding a common time is still doable, especially if you commit to planning your group times at the beginning of each term, semester, or even year. This also is a manageable number in terms of everyone having time to receive input on their writings if you choose to have hour-long meetings.

- *Five or more people.* This is treading perilously close to too many people to be worth the hassle of scheduling. Difficulty in scheduling can easily lead to procrastination of work. Before you know it, a whole term may have gone by during which little or no work was done simply because your group couldn't find a common time to meet. However, if you have five or more people whose availability lines up, you can make it work. Just know it may be a challenge. The larger the group, the longer you will most likely need to schedule your meetings so everyone can be heard. This may lead to meetings too long not only to schedule but also to bear.

Choosing Your Group Members

Choosing group members could be a matter of simply working with those from your department who share common research interests, or seeking out individuals you know or have heard about who are interested in scholarship but can provide a new or fresh perspective. If there's someone in your unit or department to invite, the two of you have the advantage of knowing in depth your topics of interest. On the other hand, having folks from outside your areas of expertise will provide fresh eyes and perspectives. It will also get people out of any silos.

If you are soliciting group members or have the luxury of creating more than one scholarship support group, you should also think about your current relationships with prospective group members and theirs to each other. Although friendships are important, the group is coming together for a specific purpose, so friendship needs to facilitate rather than debilitate the group's process. Here are some questions to think about: Are you too good of a friend with some people? Think hard about this one. Although it will be easier to approach a good friend about joining your group, do you think you might take that person's feedback or comments about your work personally? Will you be hesitant to give honest feedback because you fear it will negatively impact your friendship? What will you do if your friend continually misses the group meetings? Will you lead your group off topic and eat up group time because you're too busy having a conversation with your friend about what you did together last weekend? Although good friends are essential to a happy life, they may not be the wisest choice for a group such as this one.

Consider also any power differentials among possible group members and how this may impact candor and support. If your relationship with another person is that of supervisor and direct report (regardless of which one you are), this may be uncomfortable. If you are the supervisor, will you be open to critical feedback from an employee? If the direct report, will you construe your supervisor's comments as critical of your job performance?

Structuring Your Time Together

What should you and your group members do once you do get together? Some groups like to share copies of work before the designated meeting time. It may be overwhelming for a reader to respond to an entire work, so consider having each member submit only a piece of writing with a specific question soliciting comments. The key is to establish an agenda of what your group wants to accomplish, both individually and collectively. For example, when you get to the meeting, everyone can take turns giving input on each others' questions. Will your group have a facilitator? You may want to rotate a facilitator each meeting and agree on this person's role. If you have three people, ask someone to keep time so each member can have about 15 minutes to talk or to be the focus. You're right if you noticed that this adds up to only 45 minutes. Like most good classroom or one-on-one interactions in learning, a little time is needed at the beginning to see how everyone is doing, and, just as important, a little time is needed at the end to note what's going to happen next time, what people should be doing during that time, and what questions anyone may be having.

Most groups work well with this kind of structure: checking in with each other, sharing updates and asking questions about each member's work, and touching base about the next meeting. Other groups, however, may want more formality. Or they may have a common desire to learn something specific such as how to use the latest, greatest research software. If that's what your group would like to do, schedule a meeting with the librarian, who can help you with this. And don't just assign someone in your group to do it later; while you are all still together actually call or e-mail the person whose help you are seeking. This is akin to when we work with students. It's easy to tell them where they can seek help with homework or if they have concerns about accommodations for a disability. It takes a lot more energy to walk them over to the appropriate office, but it is much more effective.

℘℘℘

Most groups work well with this kind of structure:
checking in with each other, sharing updates and
asking questions about each member's work,
and touching base about the next meeting.

℘℘℘

Perhaps the most informally structured group gets together and spends their time writing rather than having an agenda that includes time for feedback or a conversation about journal selection, for example. Each person brings a laptop or paper and writes. This is a nice way to get your daily writing in as well as be in a supportive environment doing so. You may want to try this every other week or once a month. See if group members are interested and experiment. But don't forget the beginning and the end—still check in and still come to a common closing.

Using Online Groups

Proximity is one factor when creating groups. It may be more convenient to have all group members at one campus. However, if you have interested colleagues at other campuses nearby or in parts of the world far away, going digital may work. This is convenient also if you do meet in person but a group member happens to be away. Do remember about time zones when you schedule; this can be especially challenging if you are working with colleagues internationally.

Anecdotally, we have heard that for many people online meetings are not as productive or meaningful as in-person meetings. Either the slight delay in voice proved problematic because people kept talking over each other, or some felt as if they were yelling at their peers because of volume issues. Even though technology has done wonders for group communication, it still hasn't replaced the very real experience of sitting in the same room with someone else. If you do pursue the online method, make sure everyone's technology works and works well with each other's. Test a meeting before the actual meeting. We're reminded of a person who had scheduled a Skype group interview and thought she could just get online to Skype at the designated time. Little did she know that she needed an administrator at her institution to download the application and that this required scheduling an appointment for someone in tech support to come to her office. Needless to say, the interview took place without her. Lee and Boud (2003) advocate conceptualizing academic development, such as writing, as a local practice. In a study of faculty writing groups, they concluded that relationships within one institution create preferable environments because people are more familiar with everyone's context of daily work.

ເວ)ແ

Even though technology has done wonders for group communication, it still hasn't replaced the very real experience of sitting in the same room with someone else.

ເວ)ແ

Choosing the Frequency and Location of Meetings

To stay on track to meet your goals, consider meeting weekly. This may seem daunting, but the regularity of one hour per week will keep you focused. This is enough time for a small group of two to four people to check in, share briefly about their week, and provide some feedback. If you meet every other week, you may want to meet for an hour and a half. We discourage meeting less frequently than this because it could promote a bit of procrastination (not in you, of course, but a group member could wait until right before your meeting before doing any work).

In addition to how often you meet, think intentionally about where to meet if you're all working together in person. If you have one place that seats all members comfortably, then you may want to use that location. Your campus library or student union may be an option if your individual departments do not have conference areas. If the weather is pleasant, by all means go outside. We're also reminded of neighborhood family soup nights when thinking about place. The reason why these can work so well is that the onus of hosting is infrequent but regularly scheduled. Meeting at different offices on campus will get you out of yours. The "host" doesn't have to provide food or have anything else, for that matter, except the location.

Taking Advantage of Writing Retreats

If your department, division, or institution offers writing retreats, by all means sign up. These can last from one day to an entire workweek. They may be on or off campus, and they may even include overnight stays. A writing retreat is usually led by a facilitator, who may have you try writing exercises, put you in groups, or do something else to increase productivity.

Take advantage of these retreats if they are an option on your campus. If not, consider organizing one yourself. Begin with your department or unit; if you are a supervisor who supports scholarship, consider creating space and time for a half-day or daylong retreat.

What If . . . ?

When we engage in support groups it's likely that issues will crop up. Let's take a look at some of these issues and what you can do about them:

- *Someone continually misses the meetings.* Prevent this by asking people's commitment for a term rather than indefinitely. This gives people a graceful out at the end of the designated time in case groups don't work for them at this time in their lives. If they do promise to attend and then actually don't, reach out to them once or twice to encourage them to participate. If that doesn't work, let them go and focus on your own work.
- *Someone didn't meet his or her goal.* Was the goal realistic? Remember our thoughts about goal setting in chapter 5. Perhaps helping this person craft a more specific, realistic goal would be appropriate. We all have missed goals. Sharing stories of how members have missed the mark can help alleviate angst or embarrassment.
- *It's just not working out.* Give the group a finite amount of time such as a term or even a month to see if members want to make the arrangement permanent.
- *Your time turns into a gripe session or pity party.* Good facilitation brings people back to the purpose of the group. If your group rotates a facilitator, agree on the facilitator's role, which may include staying on the topic of writing. Even if you don't designate a facilitator, you may want to consider creating group norms at the outset.
- *Your entire group decides to skip a week.* If you have been meeting regularly for a good length of time and your group decides to skip a week, go ahead. If you decide to do this too early on, however, be aware of the dangers of getting back on schedule. You may also consider something like six weeks on and one week off or taking a week off that naturally falls on the calendar, such as a semester break period.
- *You want to celebrate.* By all means, work in a celebration if you stay with the group process. Meeting weekly for a month may be cause enough for celebration depending on your circumstances. Regardless of when you celebrate, be sure you do even when the victories are small.

8

THE FUTURE OF RESEARCH AND SCHOLARSHIP IN STUDENT AFFAIRS

Insights From Senior Student Affairs Officers

We know that student affairs professionals do not pursue scholarship enough through presenting and publishing and that the profession of student affairs has seen a decrease in scholarship by administrators (Saunders, Register, Cooper, Bates, & Daddona, 2000). In chapter 1, we explored some of the reasons that scholarship is not occurring, including working in silos and not building communities of practice, as well as not having research and scholarship valued by supervisors, which can zap staff motivation to engage (Fey & Carpenter, 1996; Saunders & Cooper, 1999; Schroeder & Pike, 2001). Senior student affairs officers (SSAOs) understand the importance, now more than ever, of sharing what student affairs professionals contribute to student learning and development with students, parents, and other invested stakeholders.

In a time of rising education costs and diminishing funds supplied by both the state and federal government, universities are being asked to provide evidence of educational quality and student accessibility. Parents and students alike are questioning the worth of a college degree given the enormous costs to students. Are students prepared for life, work, and civic engagement as a result of attaining a college degree? What are the employment opportunities for students once they graduate? Are colleges and universities equitable and fair? To help answer these questions, SSAOs must create cultures for research and scholarship. Otherwise, student affairs professionals will continue to be viewed as service providers rather than educators, and their work considered superfluous to the academic experience.

ℰℭ

SSAOs must create cultures for research and scholarship.

ℰℭ

We are all at various points on the continuum of presenting and publishing; some of us have never presented before and some of us have had several journal articles or books published. We commend all of you regardless of where you are on that journey. In this final chapter, however, we look specifically at the notion of scholarship as it applies to our profession of student affairs. Some people define *scholarship* as pure original and experimental research; others would say that *scholarship* can and perhaps should be practical in nature and applicable or transferable to your own situations. We believe that the scholarly process entails curiosity, some digging and research, and a conclusion or two that you've drawn from that digging that can be helpful to others in the area you are curious about. To complete that process (until the next iteration), we encourage you to present what you learned at a conference or seek to publish your findings in one of the myriad journals available.

You made it this far in reading this book, so you know that we truly value scholarship. This book would not have been possible without our collaborative efforts and without the support of our senior administrators. Now, we turn the tables just a bit to glean insight from SSAOs across the nation about how they view the current state of scholarship in student affairs, how they themselves became scholars, and what suggestions they have for others in leadership roles to advance their own scholarship and facilitate the same in their staff. We selected the following colleagues because they are in senior leadership roles and are also actively involved in presenting and publishing:

- Laura Bayless, assistant vice chancellor for Student Affairs, University of Wisconsin–Platteville
- Doris Ching, emeritus vice president for Student Affairs, University of Hawai'i System
- Michael Christakis, associate vice president for Student Success and public service professor, University at Albany, State University of New York
- Zebulun Davenport, vice chancellor for Student Affairs, Indiana University–Purdue University Indianapolis
- Kathleen Kerr, executive director of Residence Life & Housing, University of Delaware
- Jennifer Massey, assistant dean for Student Learning & Engagement, Baylor University
- Michael Segawa, vice president for Student Affairs and dean of students, University of Puget Sound

- Frank Shushok Jr., senior associate vice president for Student Affairs and associate professor of higher education, Virginia Tech

The Current State of Scholarship

The landscape of scholarship through presenting and publishing is changing for student affairs. Michael Segawa has seen the quality of presentations improve at NASPA over the three decades he has been involved in student affairs. He believes that we now have "lots more choices about what to read or who to hear from" through both ACPA and NASPA that are directly related to scholarship. However, overall, the current state of scholarship that entails digging and research can be better. "Personally, I do not think we do a good job of scholarship, presenting, and publishing," says Zebulun Davenport. He adds that many presentations at student affairs conferences lack scholarly depth, are more anecdotal, and are primarily about how programs work. Jennifer Massey concurs: "A variety of presentations I see are not scholarly bound. [There are many] more presentations about what students affairs practitioners are doing."

Kathleen Kerr sees somewhat of an evolution, however, from purely sharing program information to something that is approaching more of scholarship about the field. "It used to be that people would go to conventions and do what we call show-and-tell. They would talk about what they were doing on their campus. I don't really view that as scholarship," Kathleen says. "You have to ground it in something that provides some relevance to people for their own campuses. So what is the scholarship, research, or philosophical underpinning that [attendees] could transfer onto their own campuses, their student population, given their own resources, or cultural context?" Michael Segawa asks, "Is scholarship truly connected to our practices, and is the practice being informed by theory that is generated? I don't think those linkages are consistent and as strong as they need to be yet."

ഇറോ

"Is scholarship truly connected to our practices, and is
the practice being informed by theory that is generated?"
Michael Segawa, University of Puget Sound

ഇറോ

What It Takes to Produce Scholarship

In talking with SSAOs who have presented and published, we hoped to learn how they found the wherewithal to share their work given the demands of their roles. What we found were people who loved their work and truly believed in the value of it. Let's take a look at the good things they shared.

- *Be curious.* What creates a love of this work? You need a curious mind that is always asking, "What if . . . ?" Michael Christakis likes the idea of taking out that pad of paper and just writing his thoughts down. For him, the ideas themselves and reflecting on how those ideas meld together are important first steps to scholarly inquiry. Michael is personally very curious about his world; he is currently writing three different pieces, but he feels student affairs as a whole is "probably a long way from where we sort of need to be with some of this." Zebulun Davenport also refers to his curious self: "I am a learner, so I love acquiring new information, and I am inquisitive."

- *Foster the right habits.* Student affairs staff are often reactive in their work so their days do not necessarily belong to them. It makes carving out time for scholarship difficult. "We're constantly drinking water out of a fire hose, so when do you pause to do that sort of writing and reading and research?" asks Michael Christakis. Good question. It did not surprise us then that time (or lack thereof) was mentioned not only frequently but also immediately by everyone we interviewed as the main reason senior student affairs leaders do not pursue scholarship. "There are a lot of us that do a lot of presenting and attending conferences when we are able to, but finding the time to write is something I think is the most challenging piece," says Kathleen Kerr.

  How then do these SSAOs manage to engage with current practices and theories? Through the *daily* integration of reading and writing. In other words, reading and writing are not extra work; they are part of the work. Frank Shushok says carving out time to write, teach, and read is an obstacle but one that he is willing to confront. Frank believes that others think he reads all the time but he actually reads as little as 10 to 15 minutes a night. However, those minutes quickly add up. The mantra of a little bit every day can also be applied to Frank's writing, he says.

  "The way I frame the thought of being a scholar practitioner is not to bifurcate it, to not view it as something separate from the work that I do on a daily basis. I mesh the two together," says Kathleen Kerr. "I role model for my staff that we all have to be scholar practitioners, making sure that the decisions of my department and the decisions of staff are driven by good scholarship."

ഇര

"I role model for my staff that we all have to be scholar practitioners, making sure that the decisions of my department and the decisions of staff are driven by good scholarship." Kathleen Kerr, University of Delaware

ഇര

- *Find a mentor.* Whether in a graduate program or in one's current work, having a mentor has been invaluable for many of the SSAOs we talked to. "We are so much a product of what we're taught," says Frank Shushok of the mentoring he received at both the master's and doctoral levels. He continues this legacy of mentoring as he writes papers with his own graduate students, repeating the pattern modeled for him, which included writing a book chapter with his dissertation adviser. Frank is modeling the culture from which he came, the culture that acculturated him. He attributes his adviser to teaching him that "being a scholar and a practitioner are not mutually exclusive things; in fact, they inform one another."

  Zebulun Davenport says, "[I have always] paired myself up with individuals who do what I want to do." He adds that in seeking growth and development "[I have always been] practicing and putting myself in places where I can learn from people who are doing the things that I want to do."

  Jennifer Massey came into student affairs via a circuitous and more academic path, one that was heavily research focused. She transitioned into student affairs as an assessment professional and was hired because of her research skills. Jennifer has had a student affairs vice president who gave her a lot of freedom to pursue scholarship. "He encouraged me to publish my work, develop collaborative partnerships with academic colleagues on campus, and it really just started this trajectory that I have continued." She adds, "So, a combination of an unusual student affairs background, coupled with a really strong research background, and great mentoring have made all the difference."

What Can Leaders Do to Foster Scholarship?

These SSAOs shared many personal examples and ideas for promoting scholarship in their staff, ideas that other leaders can use. And for a few of these ideas, they admit when they are tough to implement.

- *Be a role model.* Pursuing presenting and publishing does not stop when the job does. "I think I'm doing more scholarship after I retired!" exclaims Doris Ching. After retiring, Doris helped found the Asian Pacific Islander Research Coalition in 2012 and has coedited a book about Asian Pacific Americans in student affairs.

  Kathleen Kerr underscores the importance of doing and not just talking:

  > I think it's important to have that mental framework—that scholarship has to be an important part of our daily work, of our practice. I need to believe it, say it, role model it, and then hold my staff members to that expectation as we make decisions that affect students. We should always be immersed in understanding what scholarship exists, no matter how busy we are. We read the *Chronicle*, we read *About Campus* and the *Journal of College Student Development*, attend conferences and institutes, and give back to the profession in a scholarly way when we can.

- *Foster collaborations.* Frank Shushok says he always has a writing project going on, typically with someone else. When working with another person, there is a sense of responsibility to that person, which helps keep him accountable. "Writing is such a great way to stay connected to colleagues," he says. Zebulun Davenport partners with academic affairs and uses student affairs "labs" with academic curriculum and content. We must "articulate what we are teaching students in the language of the academy. As student affairs professionals we do not do that," he says.

  When he was approached to write a book with a colleague, Zebulun jumped right in. He had never done this before but he wanted to learn about it:

  > I wanted to put what I had gained through my journey out there for others because I felt like it could be helpful. I felt like there was information from which other professionals could benefit. After that experience, I started asking others that I knew who were publishing about co-authoring, researching, and writing, and one thing led to the next. It was really about seeking out the opportunities and also finding people who could mentor me.

- *Encourage your staff.* In addition to modeling the pursuit of scholarship, Kathleen Kerr advocates SSAOs actively encouraging their staffs to pursue publishing and presenting opportunities. This may entail allowing time during the workday to write and supporting a flexible schedule in order to do so. Zebulun Davenport also supports alternative work schedules and flextime to allow for research and writing, "providing the space for this work."

When supervisors not only encourage but also expect their staff to contribute to student affairs research, the latter have even more motivation to present and publish. Jennifer Massey has worked at institutions that had varying feelings toward contributing to the field. However, when it was an institution's expectation, she was given the time to devote to it. At other campuses, scholarship was considered something "nice to do," but it was difficult for student affairs professionals to pursue scholarship because they were not evaluated on it and thus it was not given as much weight as their other job responsibilities.

Michael Christakis's staff is open to presenting but some need a bit more encouragement. "They need to be encouraged to spend the effort, and they need to be allowed the time in their work life to do it," he says. "And they need to be given a perspective on the value of their work, that what they are doing is worthy of being shared with others. We tend to be a humble profession." Creating an organizational culture that values scholarship is necessary, says Frank Shushok, "because this is good for the institution and for student affairs, and it represents the kind of student affairs work we hope to do."

- *Create systems to nurture scholarship.* Leaders can encourage their staff to and even create expectations that they will contribute to the field in some way. However, if organizational systems are not in place for this to be successful, staff may be perennially frustrated. In addition to allowing for flexible schedules when staff can engage with reading, writing, or researching, leaders can implement other organizational frameworks to promote these activities.

"An important first step in this notion of inquiry is reading," says Michael Christakis. "This can be reading a journal article, a blog post, anything that further refines your interest to dive a little deeper." Michael's own vice president is an avid reader about the profession of student affairs.

If staff or divisions have common readings or common guiding questions for exploration, then this creates an expectation of knowledge sharing. Zebulun Davenport notes "intentionality" at Indiana University–Purdue University Indianapolis, where his division has a common set of research questions that everyone can use when they want to measure impact on desired outcomes from their various interventions. Kathleen Kerr's department at the University of Delaware studies six topics over the course of a year. Her graduate students and staff examine these topics in a scholarly way and think about how best practices in association with these topics will inform their strategic planning process in the subsequent year. Topics have included gender violence and alcohol use, the sophomore experience, underrepresented students' experiences, and retention issues on college campuses. Her staff looks at these topics from a big-picture and scholarly perspective and asks how they apply to her campus. "I think that is one way senior officers can empower their staff to keep them in touch with the scholarship, but in many ways staff will be practicing their own scholarship," she says. "We might write some white papers out of this worthy of publication in one form or another. And it will inform good work we will do throughout the coming years."

Advancing the Field of Student Affairs

The SSAOs we spoke with have a wealth of experience and wisdom in contributing to the vibrant, necessary, and integral profession of student affairs. Their words and perspectives underscore the importance of student affairs professionals viewing themselves as scholar practitioners. To facilitate such self-perspectives, organizations must have systemic structures in place that allow for this. We advocate for the following:

- *Create organizational expectations.* Expectations of contributing to the field need to be in position descriptions of many jobs in student affairs because such scholarship is part of "what it means to be good at this work," says Frank Shushok. According to Jennifer Massey, "If we really want student affairs to become and emerge as a really dynamic, critical enterprise, we really need to start thinking about how we nurture that." She adds:

  > It has to be critical to what they do. . . . If you want to nurture scholarship within the division, [SSAOs] need to hire a handful of people who are like-minded because it fosters itself. If there are only one or two individuals within a division who like to write, publish, present, it becomes increasingly challenging for them to do so because it is a minority activity.

  Moreover, if student affairs leaders expect staff to present and publish, they must provide professional development to do so, which could include coaching, workshops, and webinars so that staff can improve in these areas.

- *Foster scholarly identity for new professionals.* The thinking for some goes that new professionals need time to become grounded in their functional areas. Let them learn how residence life works before *adding* the notion or expectation of scholarship. However, if we want people to view themselves as scholar practitioners, we need to foster this from the beginning of their professional careers. According to Frank Shushok, our patterns are based on what we are taught to value early on in our graduate programs and our careers, with these messages coming from faculty, colleagues, and the organizational context. These patterns and habits then become the way in which we live much of our careers. Frank asks his students these questions: "What kind of habits do you want to have? How do you want to view yourself? What does a scholar practitioner look like to you? Is that something you're going to aspire toward? What habits are you going to create to help you move in that direction?" In this sense, the very first job one has in the profession is crucial to developing that pattern.

∞℞

If we want people to view themselves as scholar practitioners, we need to foster this from the beginning of their professional careers.

∞℞

- *Provide professional development.* Laura Bayless emphasized the importance of providing professional development at all levels for student affairs staff but admitted that "it can be complicated for senior student affairs administrators to find professional development opportunities that meet their [staff] needs." We suggest that divisions consider developing an employee learning agenda for student affairs staff, thus providing opportunities for skill development in the areas of assessment, research, and scholarship.
- *Reward scholarship.* Doris Ching made it a priority to have money set aside for travel and other costs when it came to presenting or publishing for her staff. If she thought a conference proposal would benefit the division or campus, she would help fund it. That kind of support as well as having a model for promotion and tenure similar to that of our colleagues in academic affairs would "encourage participation in national organizations because that's where they get inspired," Doris says of student affairs professionals. At the University of Hawai'i–Manoa, the division of student affairs has tenure-track positions with titles of assistant, associate, and full specialist. Unfortunately, monetary or titular rewards are often lacking. "There's nothing necessarily in my role as an [associate

vice president] at a public research university that is incentivized for me to engage in any kind of scholarly research, and the same can be said of any of my colleagues and the staff that I supervise," says Michael Christakis. If leadership truly values scholarship and it is expected of positions, then it must be rewarded and in a way that is meaningful to the profession and culture of the institution.

- *Work with graduate programs.* More scholarship done by student affairs practitioners will inform graduate programs in higher education. "I think that some of the higher education student affairs master's degrees and [doctoral] programs vary significantly with their regard of emphasis on research," says Jennifer Massey. "Some programs don't emphasize research, so graduate students are not trained for this work." Student affairs practitioners can be instrumental in shaping curricula in higher education programs because they are the ones in contact with students every day.

  Every institution where Frank Shushok has worked has had a graduate program in higher education. Thus, doctoral students are thinking about things to write about, as are faculty. The stronger the partnership between the division of student affairs and the graduate program, the more collaboration and exposure to each other occurs, Frank says. As a result, the ethos is elevated to value the scholar practitioner. Laura Bayless, on the other hand, finds that teaching regularly helps her to keep thinking about best practices, keep up with the research, and be able to apply and share that research. She says there are lots of opportunities for practitioners to teach part-time. "I find in the semesters when I'm actually teaching in some ways I'm thinking more strategically, and I get more inspiration for presenting at special conferences."

- *Promote scholarship at conferences.* Anecdotally, student affairs professionals love to go to conferences. Who wouldn't? They provide concentrated opportunities to connect with colleagues, learn about what others in the field are doing, and grow professionally. However, conference organizers can do a better job of conveying the importance of scholarship in the profession. In other words, they must convey the importance of applying theory to our practice. The two largest student affairs organizations, NASPA and ACPA, have the potential to impact greatly how scholarship is perceived in the profession. As we noted in chapter 1, these organizations have had good starts at this; now, the momentum needs to keep moving forward. Although all of the SSAOs we spoke with acknowledged the importance of these and other professional organizations, many would like to see more research shared at conferences. The majority of sessions remain "feel-good stuff" or "programmatic show-and-tell." Lacking is application of theory or transferability to other contexts.

We encourage NASPA, ACPA, and other student affairs organizations to revisit the importance of scholarship in student affairs through panel discussions, workshops, and critical reviews of conference proposals that ask for theoretical frameworks and their application to presentations.

What we discovered through all of our conversations is that SSAOs are on very similar pages when it comes to scholarship in the field. Their perceptions are keen in that they agree with what the actual scholarship tells us. According to Sriram and Oster (2012), student affairs leaders "should advocate for the importance of applying research in practice, encouraging supervisees to make research a priority, and to take the time to engage scholarship regularly" (p. 391). We call on all student affairs leaders and practitioners as well as institutions and national organizations to promote such scholarship in the field. It can only improve what we do and, ultimately, improve the experiences of the students we serve daily. Isn't that, after all, why we do the work we do?

Closing Thoughts

As we noted in chapter 1, educational philosopher John Dewey talks a great deal about reflection as necessary for learning to occur. We take a few moments here to think about our experience of putting these words on paper for you to read. Why would we want to do such a thing when we have so many other responsibilities? We learned so much from everyone we spoke with for this chapter, but Doris Ching summarizes best why we decided to write this book: "I just still have a passion for a cause whether it's women or students or student affairs or Asian Americans or students in general. It's this passion for a cause that keeps me interested in scholarship." We have a passion for good scholarship and for advancing the vital work that student affairs practitioners do every day to improve the lives of thousands of students nationwide.

We hope that you will consider viewing yourself as a scholar practitioner if you don't already do so. We wish you the very best in finding your own passion and voice, and in intentionally creating your own journey in becoming a scholarly practitioner.

REFERENCES

ACPA. (2014). *Suggestions for writing a good proposal.* Retrieved from http://convention .myacpa.org/indy2014/program/program-information/

ACPA & NASPA. (2010). *Professional competency areas for student affairs practitioners.* Retrieved from http://www.naspa.org/images/uploads/main/Professional _Competencies.pdf

Agron, M. (2012). *WebinarReady: A step-by-step guide to hosting successful webinars.* Retrieved from http://webattract.com/docs/ebook/WebinarReady_eBook_july 2012.pdf

Allen, K. E. (2002). The purpose of scholarship, redefining meaning for student affairs. *NASPA Journal, 39*(2), 147–157.

American Psychological Association (APA). (2010). *Publication manual of the American Psychological Association* (6th ed.). Washington, DC: Author.

Anderson, M. H. (2010, January). Tips for effective webinars. *eLearn Magazine.* Retrieved from http://eLearnmag.acm.org/featured.cfm?aid=1710034

Ballenger, B. (2004). *The curious researcher: A guide to writing research papers* (4th ed.). New York, NY: Pearson Education.

Barr, C., & Yahoo! Inc. (2010). *The Yahoo! style guide: The ultimate sourcebook for writing, editing, and creating content for the digital world.* New York, NY: Yahoo!/ St. Martin's Griffin.

Belcher, W. L. (2009). *Writing your journal article in 12 weeks: A guide to academic publishing success.* Thousand Oaks, CA: Sage.

Bocco, D. (2012). The 10 habits of successful writers [Kindle]. doi:8532932-2929117

Boice, R. (1990). *Professors as writers: A self-help guide to productive writing* [Kindle]. doi:7337900-2049166

Boyer, E. L. (1990). *Scholarship reconsidered: Priorities of the professoriate.* Princeton, NJ: Carnegie Foundation for the Advancement of Teaching.

Boyle Single, P. (2010). *Demystifying dissertation writing.* Sterling, VA: Stylus.

Bruning, R. H., Schraw, G. J., & Ronning, R. R. (1995). *Cognitive psychology and instruction* (2nd ed.). Englewood Cliffs, NJ: Prentice Hall.

Caffarella, R. S., & Barnett, B. G. (2000). Teaching doctoral students to become scholarly writers: The importance of giving and receiving critiques. *Studies in Higher Education, 25*(1), 40–52.

Carpenter, S. (2001). Student affairs scholarship (re?)considered: Toward a scholarship of practice. *Journal of College Student Development, 42*(4), 301–318.

Carroll, B (2010). *Writing for digital media* [Kindle]. Retrieved from http://www .amazon.com/Writing-Digital-Media-Brian-Carroll-ebook/dp/B003FC9QYQ/ ref=tmm_kin_title_0

The Chicago Manual of Style (6th ed.). (2010). Chicago, IL: University of Chicago Press.

Clandinin, D. J., & Connelly, F. M. (2000). *Narrative inquiry: Experience and story in qualitative research.* San Francisco, CA: Jossey-Bass.

Clark, R. P. (2006). *Writing tools: 50 essential strategies for every writer.* New York, NY: Little, Brown and Company.

Communiqué Conferencing. (2003). *Conducting a webinar: A step-by-step guide to planning and executing a successful Webinar* [White paper]. Retrieved from http://www.communiqueconferencing.com/webseminarwhitepaper.pdf

Council for the Advancement of Standards in Higher Education. (2012). *CAS professional standards for higher education* (8th ed.). Washington, DC: Author.

Creswell, J. W. (1998). *Qualitative inquiry and research design: Choosing among five traditions.* Thousand Oaks, CA: Sage.

Creswell, J. W. (2003). *Research design: Qualitative, quantitative, and mixed methods approaches* (2nd ed.). Thousand Oaks, CA: Sage.

Deci, E. L., & Ryan, R. M. (1992). The initiation and regulation of intrinsically motivated learning and achievement. In A. K. Boggiano & T. S. Pittman (Eds.), *Achievement and motivation: A social developmental perspective* (pp. 3–36). Toronto, Canada: Cambridge University Press.

Denzin, N. K., & Lincoln, Y. S. (Eds.). (2000). *Handbook of qualitative research* (2nd ed.). Thousand Oaks, CA: Sage.

Dewey, J. (1902). *Child and the curriculum.* Chicago, IL: University of Chicago Press.

Dewey, J. (1910). *How we think.* Boston, MA: D.C. Heath & Co.

Dilley, P., & Hart, J. (2009, Winter). Writing for publication. *Developments.* Retrieved from http://www.myacpa.org/publications/developments/volume-7-issue-4

Dweck, C. S. (2006). *Mindset: The new psychology of success.* New York, NY: Ballantine Books.

Fey, C. J., & Carpenter, D. S. (1996). Mid-level student affairs administrators: Management skills and professional development needs. *NASPA Journal, 33*(3), 218–231.

Fripp, P. (2009, July). 15 tips for webinars. *eLearn Magazine.* Retrieved from http://elearnmag.acm.org/featured.cfm?aid=1595445

Gardner, S., & Birley, S. (2010). *Blogging for dummies.* Indianapolis, IN: Wiley.

Gould, M. (2013, October 2). Writing online content (excerpt from the social media gospel) [Blog]. Retrieved from http://meredithgould.blogspot.com/2013/10/writing-online-content-excerpt-from.html

Gregory, H. (1999). *Public speaking for college and career.* New York, NY: McGraw-Hill College.

Hobson, E. H. (2001). Writing center pedagogy. In G. Tate, A. Rupiper, & K. Schick (Eds.), *A guide to composition studies* (pp. 165–182). New York, NY: Oxford University Press.

Hoff, R. (1988). *I can see you naked: A fearless guide to making great presentations.* Kansas City, MO: Andrews and McMeel.

Jablonski, M. A., Mena, S. B., Manning, K., Carpenter, S., & Siko, K. L. (2006). Scholarship in student affairs revisited: The summit on scholarship, March 2006. *NASPA Journal, 43*(4), 182–201.

Keith, W., & Lundberg, C. O. (2014). *Public speaking: Choices and responsibility.* Boston, MA: Wadsworth.

Kidder, R. (2010, Spring). Part 1: The scholar practitioner: Administrators engaging in the research process. *Developments.* Retrieved from http://www.myacpa.org/publications/developments/volume-8-issue-1

Kimbrough, W. M. (2007). How did I end up here? A reflection on advancement in student affairs. In R. L. Ackerman & L. D. Roper (Eds.), *The mid-level manager in student affairs* (pp. 275–293). Washington, DC: NASPA.

Krathwohl, D. R. (2009). *Methods of educational and social science research: The logic of methods.* Long Grove, IL: Waveland Press.

Kuh, G. D., & Banta, T. W. (2000). Faculty-student affairs collaborations on assessment: Lessons from the field. *About Campus, 4*(6), 4–11.

Lee, A., & Boud, D. (2003). Writing groups, change and academic identity: Research development as local practice. *Studies in Higher Education, 28*(2), 187–200. doi:10.1080/0307507032000058109

LeechBlock. (n.d.). Retrieved from https://addons.mozilla.org/en-US/firefox/addon/leechblock/

Machi, L. A., & McEvoy, B. T. (2012). *The literature review: Six steps to success* (2nd ed.). Thousand Oaks, CA: Corwin.

Marshall, C., & Gerstl-Pepin, C. (2005). *Re-framing educational politics for social justice.* Boston, MA: Pearson.

Maxwell, J. A. (2012). *The realist approach to qualitative research.* Thousand Oaks, CA: Sage.

Mitchell, O. (2010, October 1). 18 tips on how to conduct an engaging webinar [Web log message]. Retrieved from http://www.speakingaboutpresenting.com/presentation-skills/how-to-conduct-engaging-webinar/

Modern Language Association. (2008). *MLA style manual and guide to scholarly publishing* (3rd ed.). New York, NY: Author.

Modern Language Association. (2009). *MLA handbook for writers of research papers* (7th ed.). New York, NY: Author.

Moore Howard, R. (2001). Collaborative pedagogy. In G. Tate, A. Rupiper, & K. Schick (Eds.), *A guide to composition studies* (pp. 54–70). New York, NY: Oxford University Press.

Nanny for Google Chrome. (n.d.). Retrieved from https://chrome.google.com/webstore/detail/nanny-for-google-chrome-t/cljcgchbnolheggdgaeclffeagnnmhno

NASPA Task Force on Research and Scholarship. (October, 2011). *A research and scholarship agenda for the student affairs profession.* Retrieved from http://nasparegion5.files.wordpress.com/2012/02/naspa-research-agenda.pdf

Oregon Department of Education. (n.d.). *Speaking official scoring guide 2011–2014.* Salem, OR: Author. Retrieved from http://www.ode.state.or.us/wma/teachlearn/testing/scoring/guides/2011-12/spkingscorguides1112.pdf

Peters, C., & Griffiths, K. (2012, January). 10 steps for planning a successful webinar: Tips for organizing and producing online seminars for your nonprofit or charity [Web log message]. Retrieved from http://www.techsoup.org/support/articles-and-how-tos/10-steps-for-planning-a-successful-webinar

The Royal Literary Fund. (n.d.). *What is the importance of feedback?* Retrieved from http://www.rlf.org.uk/fellowshipscheme/writing/diswriting/quotes.cfm?title=What%20is%20the%20importance%20of%20feedback%3F&table=feedback&selected=1

Saunders, S. A., & Cooper, D. L. (1999). The doctorate in student affairs: Essential skills and competencies for midmanagement. *Journal of College Student Development, 40*(2), 185–191.

Saunders, S. A., Register, M. D., Cooper, D. L., Bates, J. M., & Daddona, M. F. (2000). Who is writing research articles in student affairs journals? Practitioner involvement and collaboration. *Journal of College Student Development, 41*(6), 609–615.

Schroeder, C. C., & Pike, G. R. (2001). The scholarship of application in student affairs. *Journal of College Student Development, 42*(4), 342–355.

Seinfeld, J. (1998). *I'm telling you for the last time* [Video file]. Retrieved from http://www.youtube.com/watch?v=kL7fTLjFzAg

Sense About Science. (2009). *Peer review survey 2009*. Retrieved from http://www.senseaboutscience.org/pages/peer-review-survey-2009.html

Sermersheim, K. L., & Keim, M. C. (2005). Mid-level student affairs managers: Skill importance and need for continued professional development. *The College Student Affairs Journal, 25*(1), 36–49.

Silvia, P. J. (2007). *How to write a lot: A practical guide to productive academic writing.* Washington, DC: American Psychological Association.

SMART criteria. (n.d.). In *Wikipedia, The Free Encyclopedia.* Retrieved from http://en.wikipedia.org/wiki/SMART_goals

Sriram, R. (2011). *Engaging research as a student affairs professional.* NetResults. Retrieved from http://works.bepress.com/rishi_sriram/10

Sriram, R., & Oster, M. (2012). Reclaiming the "scholar" in scholar-practitioner. *Journal of Student Affairs Research and Practice, 49*(4), 377–396. doi:10.1515/jsarp-2012-6432

Tashakkori, A., & Teddlie, C. (Eds.). (2003). *Handbook of mixed methods in the social and behavioral sciences.* Thousand Oaks, CA: Sage.

Torrance, M., & Galbraith, M. (2006). The processing demands of writing. In C. A. MacArthur, S. Graham, & J. Fitzgerald (Eds.), *Handbook of writing research* (pp. 67–80). New York, NY: Guilford Press.

Torrance, M., Thomas, G. V., & Robinson, E. J. (1992). The writing experiences of social science research students. *Studies in Higher Education, 17*(2), 155–167. doi:10.1080/03075079212331382637

Upcraft, M. L., & Schuh, J. H. (1996). *Assessment in student affairs: A guide for practitioners.* San Francisco, CA: Jossey-Bass.

Wang, S., & Hsu, H. (2008). Use of the webinar tool (Elluminate) to support training: The effects of webinar-learning implementation from student-trainers' perspective. *Journal of Interactive Online Learning, 7*(30), 175–194. Retrieved from www.ncolr.org/jio

Wiggins, G. P. (1998). *Educative assessment: Designing assessments to inform and improve student performance.* San Francisco, CA: Jossey-Bass.

Wise, V. L., Spiegel, A. N., & Bruning, R. H. (1999). Using teacher reflective practice to evaluate professional development in mathematics and science. *Journal of Teacher Education, 50*(1), 42–49.

Wolcott, H. F. (2001). *Writing up qualitative research.* Thousand Oaks, CA: Sage.

Zinsser, W. (2006). *On writing well* (7th ed.). New York, NY: Collins.

"Given today's complex and ever-changing life demands, *Authoring Your Life* offers a timely, crucial map of possibilities for helping ourselves and others to grow and to meet the implicit and explicit demands of post-modern life. In a highly accessible manner, Baxter Magolda consciously, thoughtfully, and gently teaches us about her robust 'cyclical model' for how to authentically grow from life's challenges and experiences through what she calls 'learning partnerships.' By sharing real life experiences from courageous adults, and how they made sense of and navigated their way through them, she illuminates the internal landscape of personal growth as a developmental process. This book, informed by constructive-developmental theory, will enable us to nurture adult development."

—***Ellie Drago-Severson,***
Associate Professor of Education Leadership,
Teachers College, Columbia University,
and author of Helping Teachers Learn and Leading Adult Learning

Sty/us

22883 Quicksilver Drive
Sterling, VA 20166-2102   Subscribe to our e-mail alerts: www.Styluspub.com

Also available from Stylus

The Strategic Guide to Shaping Your Student Affairs Career
Sonja Ardoin
Foreword by Marcia B. Baxter Magolda

"*The Strategic Guide to Shaping Your Student Affairs Career* is a one-of-a-kind resource for student affairs administrators in any stage of their career. The book is well organized around five key elements of career strategy that helpfully prompt readers to not only focus and reflect on critical stages in their career development and advancement, but also on their personal motivations and goals. This is enhanced by the inclusion of voices of current administrators who share their stories and insights to illustrate the book's message."

—Ashley Tull,
Director of Assessment and Strategic Initiatives,
Division of Student Affairs, Southern Methodist University

"This book fills a huge hole in the field of student affairs—namely, helping graduate students and new professionals chart a path for their career. The writing is crisp and clean, and very easy to read. By taking a strategic approach to identifying career goals and planning a deliberate approach to one's own professional development, Dr. Ardoin's book is a clear and useful guide to the profession. It will be very useful in teaching graduate students how to think about the future, but is also useful as a guide for the new professional in their first or second job who is thinking, 'What is next and how do I get there?!' A great contribution by Ardoin and her many contemporaries who share their own stories of success."

—Robert A. Schwartz,
Professor of Higher Education and Chair,
Department of Educational Leadership and Policy Studies, Florida State University

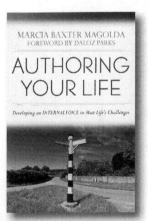

Authoring Your Life
Developing an Internal Voice to Navigate Life's Challenges
Marcia B. Baxter Magolda
Illustrated by Matthew Henry Hall
Foreword by Sharon Daloz Parks

"This book should be considered an essential addition to the library for the young professional just entering a career in academic advising. The emphasis placed on developing the skills to become a more independent thinker is essential to understanding the needs of college and university students who are in the early stages of understanding the complexities of becoming successful contributors to society as a whole."

—NACADA Journal
(National Academic Advising Association)

(Continues on previous page)